hotels • restaurants • shops • spas

tokyochic

hotels • restaurants • shops • spas

tokyochic

text tom baker • zoë jaques • mariko usuba owen

·K·U·P·E·R·A·R·D·

executive editor
melisa teo
senior editor
joanna greenfield
assistant editor
priscilla chua
designers
annie teo • **norreha sayuti**
production manager
sin kam cheong

designed and produced by
editions didier millet pte ltd
121 telok ayer street, #03-01
singapore 068590
email: edm@edmbooks.com.sg
website: www.edmbooks.com

first published in great britain 2007 by
kuperard
59 hutton grove, london n12 8ds
telephone : +44 (0) 20 8446 2440
facsimile : +44 (0) 20 8446 2441
enquiries : sales@kuperard.co.uk
website   : www.kuperard.co.uk

Kuperard is an imprint of Bravo ltd.

©2007 editions didier millet pte ltd

Printed in Singapore

isbn: 978-1-85733-417-3

COVER CAPTIONS:

1, 6, 21: Luxury at the Hyatt Regency Kyoto.
2: The Conrad Tokyo's lobby.
3: Shopping in style at Roppongi Hills.
4: High fashion from Dresscamp.
5: An exhibit at the National Art Center.
7: Lunch at the Park Hotel Tokyo.
8: Modern comfort at Grand Hyatt Tokyo.
9, 20: Scenes of traditional Japanese culture.
10: Art on display at SCAI The Bathhouse.
11: Dramatic structure of the National Art Center.
12: Gordon Ramsay's Cerise brasserie.
13: Fresh sashimi from Chef Yoshihiro Murata.
14: Beautiful cherry blossom of spring.
15: A bustling intersection.
16: The traditional macha to stir green tea.
17: Simple understated style at Badou-R.
18: The mesmerising cityscape.
19: Prada's flagship on Omotesando.

PAGE 2: Tokyo's buzzing Ginza district.

THIS PAGE: A beacon of style at Roppongi Hills.

OPPOSITE: Roppongi Hills' Counter Void.

PAGE 6: Cherry blossom at Chef Murata's
Kikunoi Restaurant in Kyoto.

PAGE 8 AND 9: In neon-lit Shinjuku, Yasukuni-dori
pulses with life.

contents

Japan Sea

Kanazawa

3180 Yariga-take ▲

2702 ▲

3063 Ontake-san ▲

CHUBU

H o n s h u

Wakasa-wan

3776
Fuji-san ▲

Biwa-ko

Kyoto

Nagoya

Ise-
wan

Suruga-wan

Osaka

KINKI

Nara

Legend

Highway
Main Road
Shinkansen
Airport
Water
3000–4000 m
2000–3000 m
1000–2000 m
500–1000 m
200–500 m

▲
1915

0 km   25   50   75 km

N

tokyo+surroundings

Kashima-nada

KANTO

Kasumiga-ura

Tokyo

Yokohama

Kamakura

Sagami-nada

kone

Pacific Ocean

• Nikko

tokyo+surroundingsbychapter

Tokyo in the Hills

Tokyo
by the Water

Beyond Tokyo
Hakone

nd Tokyo
yoto

introduction

The rising sun touches the tops of Tokyo's tallest towers first. Then, the morning light spreads downward and into the streets as another day begins. Some things look the same with each dawn—seafood dealers haggling at the fish market, commuters reading the morning papers on the train, pigeons beginning to stir on the grounds of an old temple—but something is always different. Japan's nickname, Land of the Rising Sun, is especially apt in Tokyo, as each day's sunrise reveals something new. Dozens more high-rise buildings have gone up in recent years, catching the morning rays a few seconds earlier with each new girder put in place.

The people on the street are always changing, too. In early January, the sun might shine down on worshippers making their hatsumode, or first New Year's visit to a temple or shrine, just as they and their neighbours have done for as long as anyone can remember. But on other days those same people will greet the dawn at the end of a night spent on the pavement outside an electronics superstore in hopes of being the first in their neighbourhood to own the latest hot gadget.

As the sun moves higher, more new sights are revealed, chic Tokyoites step out in fashions that weren't seen last week and stop in at shops and restaurants that didn't exist a month ago. At night, when an explosion of neon replaces the sun and the building façades turn into giant video screens, when party people converge at various clubs snapping each other's photos on their mobile phones, and when homeward bound commuters are watching movies rather than reading newspapers, the sensation of newness pervades everything.

But even in ever-changing Tokyo, not all is new. Red paper lanterns are as easy to find as Blu-ray disks. Traditional yatai street food stalls roll into place for the night around the corner from trendy new bistros. People who ride moving sidewalks through cavernous train stations in the latest designer shoes also enjoy padding across a traditional tatami floor in their socks when they get home.

Despite such comforting threads of continuity, you can bet your last yen that when the sun rises tomorrow, it won't be seeing quite the same Tokyo it set on last night.

THIS PAGE: *Tokyo's growing legion of skyscrapers, such as this one in Shibuya, offer a chance to get above it all for a big-picture view.*
OPPOSITE: *The thronging Shibuya area, especially the famous crosswalk in front of its main rail station, is an excellent venue for people-watching.*

tokyo's edo roots

Tokyo is a relatively young city. From its roots as a backwater fishing town named Edo, it rose to historic significance a scant four centuries ago. Ieyasu Tokugawa, a shogun who came to power after a long period of national instability, moved the capital from Kyoto to Edo in 1603. This dramatic change was a fresh start in both real and symbolic terms.

The government he established defined the Edo era (1603–1867), during which 15 Tokugawa shoguns ruled Japan from the city. Maintaining peace through a firm grip on power, the shoguns set up a system of alternate residence in which the nation's daimyos, lords of domains around the country, would divide their time between Edo and their own territories. The daimyo's wives and children were required to live in Edo, essentially as hostages to the shogun. Beyond its political uses, this arrangement contributed to the growth of the city, as luxurious residences were built and vast streams of people and goods flowed in and out. A wealthy merchant class arose, and artists and craftsmen found plenty of demand for their work. It was then that kabuki theatre flourished, providing entertainment for the masses.

Life in Edo offered its share of delights, but harsh laws, rigid social stratification and unyielding codes of honour kept everyone in their place. Order was further maintained by the nearly absolute exclusion of foreign influences. But in 1853, US Navy Commodore Matthew Perry sailed into Tokyo Bay to demand that Japan negotiate an opening to American trade. The arrival of his Black Ships on Edo's doorstep created a sensation, especially since Japan's isolation had caused it to miss the Industrial Revolution. The noisy, smoking steamships were like nothing the people had ever seen. They foreshadowed a major national transformation.

Factions for and against engaging with foreigners emerged, and fighting among them led to the 1868 Meiji Restoration. The last shogun abdicated, and the teenaged Emperor Mutsuhito (or Meiji, as he is now known) was brought from Kyoto to Edo to head a new government. Underlining the change, the capital was renamed. Feudal old Edo became forward-looking Tokyo.

During the Meiji period (1868–1912), Japan and its renamed capital advanced at a furious pace. Scholars were sent abroad, technical experts were invited from overseas, a written constitution was enacted, an elected Diet was convened, industries were built and Western-style buildings became a part of the Tokyo cityscape.

But along with all the positive trappings of modernity, Japan also acquired a taste for foreign military adventures, taking control of Taiwan and other areas in the 1894–5 Sino-Japanese War. Ten years later, Japan gained more territory in the Russo-Japanese War of 1904–5, and in 1910 Japan annexed Korea.

After Meiji's death, his son Yoshihito (posthumously known as Taisho) took the throne for the 1912–26 Taisho period. A sickly man who died prematurely, Taisho was not an active emperor, but his brief reign was a period of continued national progress, including a movement for broader democracy that led to the adoption of universal male suffrage. Sadly, the Taisho years were marred by the Great Kanto Earthquake of 1923. The quake and subsequent fire levelled much of Tokyo and killed 100,000 people.

Among the few structures to survive the disaster were Tokyo Station, a sprawling redbrick complex that opened in 1914, and Frank Lloyd Wright's ornate Imperial Hotel, which opened in 1922 and had been built on a special floating foundation so it could withstand earthquakes. Around these two buildings a new and more modern Tokyo began to rise up from the ashes and rubble.

World War II again left most of the city in ruins, but ever-resilient Tokyoites began rebuilding their metropolis during the 1945–52 Occupation, and they have rarely paused in that task ever since. (Not all progress was positive, though: Wright's hotel was demolished and replaced in the late 1960s.) Year after year, new skyscrapers

THIS PAGE (FROM LEFT): The reign of Emperor Mutsuhito (Meiji) saw Japan change from a feudal society to an industrial one; a Buddhist festival at Ikegami Honmonji temple.

OPPOSITE (FROM TOP): A traditional percussion instrument; kabuki is the most visually spectacular of Japan's indigenous performing arts.

spring up on the skyline, new developments fill the suburbs and new train lines link it all together. Luxury shops, restaurants and hotels, from the traditional to the trendy, exist in every corner of the city, with more opening all the time. The fishing town Ieyasu chose for his capital has grown up to be a bustling, gleaming and very chic metropolis.

a taste for the tragic

In the Edo period, the stress of living under a strict regime found an outlet in tragic dramas that often concluded with the heroes committing suicide due to inescapable duty or thwarted love. Two of the most famous such stories originated as 18th-century bunraku puppet plays before being adapted for the kabuki stage. Evidence of their popularity, the samurai tragedy *Chushingura* became the plot of numerous films, while *Sonezaki Love Suicide* has been staged as a flamenco musical.

Those stories are still performed at bunraku and kabuki theatres in Tokyo today, with some venues providing English-language headphone assistance. Japan's most ancient performing art, the masked and chanted drama of noh, went high-tech in 2006 when the National Noh Theatre installed video screens in the backs of seats, displaying English summaries of the dialogue and notes on the highly stylised action.

Even today, a taste for the tragic remains. The grief caused by the untimely death of a young lover—nowadays by accident or disease rather than socially mandated suicide—is a common subject of modern Japanese films. It was also a theme of the Korean TV series *Winter Sonata*, which became one of Japan's biggest hits of the 2000s, kicking off a huge Korean drama boom in Japan.

Sometimes life imitates art, as in the sad tale of Tokyo novelist Ichiyo Higuchi, whose promising career was cut short when she died of tuberculosis in 1896 at the age of 24. The writing she left behind, though, was of such high calibre that her face, forever young, now appears on Japan's 5,000 yen note. Another Tokyo novelist, Yukio Mishima, orchestrated his own tragedy. This Tokyo native and towering figure of 20th-century Japanese literature publicly committed seppuku ritual suicide in 1970 at the age of 45, leaving behind a long shelf of tragic stories about characters who also died in their prime.

But tragedy is not the only thread in modern Japanese literature. The most widely admired Japanese novelist working today is probably Haruki Murakami, whose surreal stories are known for their leavening of wry humour. Reviewing Murakami's *Kafka on the Shore*, American novelist John Updike found much to admire, despite "a bewildering overflow of possible meanings." Murakami, who ran a Tokyo jazz bar before becoming a published author, is often talked up as a candidate for the Nobel Prize in Literature.

Japanese pop fiction is also making a mark on the wider world. The works of mystery novelists Natsuo Kirino and Miyuki Miyabe have been well received abroad, while horror novelist Koji Suzuki, sometimes labelled the Stephen King of Japan, has seen his books, most notably *The Ring*, made into films in both Japan and Hollywood.

tokyo on film

Cineastes worldwide have long admired great Japanese auteurs such as Akira Kurosawa and Yasujiru Ozu, but the success of the films like *The Ring* shows Japanese film winning over the global mainstream. Takashi Shimizu's *Juon* was such a hit that Hollywood asked him to direct the English-language

THIS PAGE (FROM TOP): A kabuki actor makes up his face with striking and heroic red stripes; Kill Bill, Vol. 1 is among the recent Hollywood movies that have used Tokyo as a setting.

OPPOSITE: The rounded contours of Mori Tower at Roppongi Hills quickly became an emblem of modern-day Tokyo.

remake. More and more often, Hollywood is coming to Tokyo—or other parts of Japan—to try to capture some magic in films as diverse as *Kill Bill Vol. 1*, *Lost in Translation*, *Tokyo Drift*, and *Letters from Iwo Jima*. When it comes to old-school animation, Japan leads the world, thanks largely to Tokyo's own Studio Ghibli, the powerhouse behind director Hayao Miyazaki's enchanting films *Laputa*, *My Neighbor Totoro*, and *Princess Mononoke*. Adding to the success story, Miyazaki's Oscar-winning *Spirited Away* became one of Japan's biggest grossing films when it was released in 2001.

Many films have their star-studded Japan premieres in Tokyo, keeping the city's glamour quotient high. It peaks in autumn, when the Tokyo International Film Festival is held. Founded in 1985, the festival takes in a broad swathe of world cinema, but since 2000, it has had a rival in the Tokyo Filmex festival, considered to have a more specifically Asian focus.

woodblock to mock rock

Coloured drawings like the ones Miyazaki brings to life have long been a strength of Japanese culture. *Great Wave off Kanagawa*, a spectacular woodblock print by the 19th-century Edo artist Hokusai, is one of the world's most instantly recognisable works of art. Part of his series *36 Views of Mount Fuji*, it inspired another Edo artist, Hiroshige, to do a similarly stunning set of scenes along the Tokaido highway, from Edo to Kyoto.

The woodblock artists were chroniclers as well as creators, and the same can be said for photographer Nobuyoshi Araki, a major figure on the city's art scene today. Born in Tokyo in 1940, he has shot cityscapes and street life for decades, in addition to his more refined floral images and controversial erotic fantasies.

A craze for cuteness pervades much of Japan's commercial culture—it's difficult to think of a single product that doesn't have a cartoon mascot—and top contemporary artists get plenty of mileage out of lampooning it. Yoshitomo Nara is famous for his

THIS PAGE (FROM TOP): The Great Wave off Kanagawa *is an icon of woodblock print art;* Astro Boy, *a different kind of icon, created by Osamu Tezuka.*

OPPOSITE (FROM TOP): Ozoni *soup with mochi rice paste is the customary accompaniment to boxed* osechi *New Year's meals; two girls hold* hagoita *paddles for the badminton-like game of* hanetsuki, *a traditional New Year's holiday recreation.*

paintings of soft, round-faced little girls who somehow manage to be cute and menacing at the same time. Sculptor Takashi Murakami, meanwhile, takes the exaggerated figures typically seen in manga comic books and exaggerates them even further in 3D, with often hilarious results.

Just as Murakami and Nara take commodified art and make it new again, so do some of Japan's best popular musicians buck the trends of an often mechanical music industry. Indistinguishable manufactured teen idols come and go with each page of the calendar, but real musical talent also finds its way to the top. Two brothers billed as Yoshida Kyodai, a pair of highly trained musicians, made waves when they appeared on the scene dressed in formal kimono and playing three-stringed Tsugaru shamisen, traditional instruments from Japan's north, as if they were rock guitars.

celebrate tokyo-style

Japanese culture is finely attuned to the changing seasons, which means that a visit to Tokyo is likely to have a different flavour depending on the dates on which it is made. Shogatsu, or New Year, is the main holiday. On the night of December 31, the old year is seen out to the deep tolling of temple bells. People flock to local Buddhist temples for a turn at swinging a battering-ram-style log against the side of a thimble-shaped bronze bell that can be as big as a phone booth. Aside from shrine or temple visits, Shogatsu is spent at home with the family, relaxing and eating osechi ryori. One of the many triumphs of traditional Japanese cuisine, osechi is a colourful collection of lightly preserved fish, vegetables, seaweed, chestnuts and other goodies, artfully arranged in a stack of lacquerware boxes. Each morsel carries a symbolic wish for the new year. Gorgeous to behold and tasty to eat, osechi can take days to prepare. In lieu of the homemade variety, restaurants and department stores compete to see who can offer the most luxurious and attractive take-home osechi to gourmet Tokyoites who are pressed for time.

The second Monday in January is Coming-of-Age Day, on which large public ceremonies mark the passage into adulthood of young people turning 20. Inwardly, the freshly minted adults may be thrilled to know they are now free to drink, smoke and vote, but outwardly they try to impress the world with what chic adults they have become. A few of the young men wear dark, masculine kimono, but most appear in smartly tailored suits. As handsome as the men are, Coming-of-Age day is really the young women's chance to shine. They dazzle the eye in graceful, gorgeously patterned kimono in every colour of the rainbow, secured with intricately tied obi sashes and highlighted by a wide range of beautiful hairstyles. Given the occasion, and the January weather, it is not unusual for their kimono to be trimmed with fur. On this day, the sidewalks of Tokyo become a showcase of glamour.

THIS PAGE (FROM TOP): Young women wearing lavish kimono on Coming-of-Age day in January; these dramatically posed dolls by Yasuko Hara wear clothes made of washi paper. OPPOSITE: A duck paddles serenely through the reflections of cherry blossoms in the water.

beans and chocolate

February brings two notable holidays, one Japanese and one imported. First comes Setsubun, a day on which families literally throw beans around the house in a symbolic driving out of evil and misfortune. There are also public Setsubun festivities in which sumo wrestlers or other celebrities toss beans from the porches of temples.

The Japanese version of Valentine's Day also calls for a barrage of edible items, but in this case it is the giri choco (obligatory chocolate) women give the men in their lives, including bosses and colleagues. On White Day, one month later, the men have to return the favour, often with cookies. In the run-up to both of these holidays, Tokyo merchants unveil large displays of festively packaged sweets.

Hina Matsuri on March 3, also known as the Doll Festival or Girls' Day, is a time when exquisitely crafted dolls go on display, in both stores and homes. Displayed on a staircase-like dais, a full set of these dolls represents an emperor, an empress and about a dozen members of their court, all dressed in ancient Japanese finery. Often precious family heirlooms, these dolls are true works of art rather than everyday playthings.

cherry golden

Springtime is best known for blossoming cherry trees, and for the hanami flower viewing parties that blossom along with them at parks all over the city. Ueno Park in the northeastern part of Tokyo is the biggest and most popular hanami venue. Inokashira Park in western Tokyo is an even more picturesque spot, as it centres on a small lake reflecting the cherry trees on its banks. At any Tokyo location, you can expect large crowds, but everyone seems to remain well behaved despite the quantities of beer and sake that are often part of the festivities. Perhaps the billions of pale pink blossoms, a few of which flutter to the ground with each passing breeze, have a calming effect.

Equally certain signs of spring's arrival, at least on the streets of major Tokyo business districts such as Shinjuku or Marunouchi, are the legions of recent university graduates wearing out their best shoe leather as they move from office to office to attend job interviews. April 1 is the start of the new fiscal year, and most major Japanese companies hire a large wave of fresh employees on or around this date.

The young workers needn't wait long for their first vacation, as many businesses shut down for the April 29 to May 5 cluster of holidays known as Golden Week. Normally bustling Tokyo neighbourhoods can seem suddenly deserted, but the train stations, highways and airports are mobbed.

dancing for the dead

A more gradual and less dramatic exodus occurs during July and August, for the Bon season. All over Japan, Bon festivals are held on various dates in this period to honour the dead. As many Tokyoites originally come from other parts of the country, this is a popular time to revisit their hometowns, spend time with their families and pay tribute to their ancestors. Of course, there are also festivities in Tokyo itself, with night-time Bon dances as the highlight. With strings of lanterns illuminating a neighbourhood park, everyone in the area, regardless of age or dancing skill, joins in a rhythmic procession around a temporary tower, atop which a taiko drummer provides a half-solemn, half-jaunty beat.

Simpler summer pleasures include listening to the buzz of cicadas in a park (an incessant, hypnotic sound that inspired a famous Basho haiku), attempting to cool oneself with a traditional paper fan, or eating chilled watermelon while watching the pyrotechnics at one of the many summer fireworks displays.

THIS PAGE (FROM TOP): A pagoda reflects in Ueno's Shinobazu Pond—an isolated segment of a long-forgotten river; women participate in a nighttime Bon dance in Tokyo.

OPPOSITE: A vigorous Kodo drummer translates muscle power into music.

christmas is for lovers

The autumn season begins with a national holiday in late September to mark the autumnal equinox. (There's a spring equivalent for the vernal equinox in March.) The changing colours of autumn are a popular motif for this quiet time of year, and it's one as evident in department store window displays as on the trees in Tokyo's parks.

Then it's time to celebrate Christmas. In Japan, this is primarily a romantic holiday for couples—much more so than Valentine's Day. Tokyo hotels and restaurants pull out all stops for the big day, outdoing themselves to offer a luxurious and memorable experience for two. The focus is usually placed on a candlelit Western-style dinner, most likely French, served with fine wine and elegant silverware.

Family celebrations of Christmas in this mainly non-Christian nation consist chiefly of fathers bringing home a beautifully decorated Christmas cake—not the usual heavy fruit variety, more a light sponge with strawberries and whipped cream. There's such a frenzy of cake-buying on December 24 and 25—and such a drop-off immediately afterward—that 'old Christmas cake' used to be a disparaging term for women who remained single past the age of 25. Nowadays, so many independent-minded Japanese women are deliberately putting off marriage that the term has lost most of its sting. But to be dateless on Christmas night is still a gloomy fate.

On a lighter note, Santa doesn't bring toys to most Japanese households, but you are likely to seem him riding a scooter to deliver pizzas in his red fur suit. For a couple of days each December, Santa costumes become de rigueur in that line of work.

flavours of the world

Tokyo's prominence as a world city means the cuisines of most other nations can be found here as well, from Swedish to Sri Lankan, and Brazilian to Belarussian. There's such an open-minded attitude toward the adaptation of foreign ingredients and techniques that dishes such as teriyaki chicken pizza, or spaghetti topped with natto fermented beans, are not thought of as conscious attempts at fusion cuisine. They simply represent the way things are.

Tokyo gourmets have developed a keen appreciation for French cuisine, and Gallic superchefs such as Alain Ducasse and Joël Robuchon have opened restaurants here to serve it to them. Meanwhile, Japanese culinary stars such as Nobu Matsuhisa and Yoshihiro Murata are showing the world what Japan has to offer.

Sushi and sashimi are a big part of that, of course, but deep red slabs of freshly caught bonito or glistening orange spoonfuls of sea urchin are only the beginning. While Tokyo is a great place for seafood, it is also the capital of a very mountainous country. From the forested inland areas there come chestnuts, pumpkins, burdock, bamboo shoots, sansai mountain vegetables, and enough different mushrooms to keep a botanist happily busy for years. And then there is the fruit—from crisp mountain pears bursting with sweet juice to 10,000-yen melons that qualify as objets d'art as much as food (although they are delicious).

Moreover, Japan's regional cuisines—all on offer in Tokyo—reflect a wide variety of climate and terrain. Japan's land area is 54 per cent larger than that of the UK, and it stretches across more than 20 degrees of latitude. Consequently, Hokkaido, in the chilly north, contributes grilled mutton to the national feast, while the signature dish of subtropical Okinawa is goya champuru, a scrambled mixture of eggs, pork, tofu and goya bitter melon. With springtime vegetables and grilled summer eel giving way to matsutake mushrooms in the autumn and Hiroshima oysters in winter, Japanese menus reflect the changing and dramatic seasons. Another part of daily life showcasing the seasonal wonder of Tokyo and the land it lies in.

THIS PAGE (FROM TOP): The elegant presentation of a kaiseki meal; chefs Nobu Matsuhisa (left) and Yoshihiro Murata (right) have made Japanese culinary techniques an important part of international haute cuisine.

OPPOSITE: Restaurant patrons cast their shadows on the wall in a fleeting vision of wabi, the Japanese aesthetic of beauty in austere simplicity.

...showcasing the seasonal wonder of Tokyo and the land it lies in.

tokyo by the water

Mejiro

Takadanobaba

Shinokubo

Shinjuku

Yoyogi

Harajuku

Shibuya

Ebisu

Meguro

Shinagawa

SCAI The Bathhouse

Ueno Park
Tokyo Metropolitan Museum of Art
Kototoi-dori

The National Museum
of Western Art, Tokyo

Ueno

The Ueno Royal Museum

Sensoji Temple

Asahi Breweries
Head Office

Akihabara

Metropolitan Expressway

> Mandarin Oriental Tokyo
> Mango Tree Tokyo

Mitsukoshimae

Otemachi

Nihonbashi

Tokyo
Station

Sotobori-dori

Chuo-dori

Marunouchi

Yuraku-cho

> Four Seasons Hotel Tokyo
  at Marunouchi
> Beige
> Atelier Shinji
> Ito-ya

> The Peninsula Tokyo
> My Humble House Tokyo
> Tasaki Shinju
> Fukumitsuya
> le 6eme sens d'OENON
> Il Pinolo
> L'Osier

Ginza

Showa-dori

Kabukiza

Tsukiji

Sumidagawa River

Sotobori-dori

Shinbashi

Hibiya-dori

Shin-Ohashi-dori

Harumidori

Tsukiji
Market

> Park Hotel Tokyo
> Conrad Tokyo
> The Oregon Bar & Grill
> Sky

Hamamatsucho

Tamachi

Metropolitan Expressway

*Tokyo
Bay*

Metropolitan Expressway

Legend

	Expressway
	Main roads
	JR Line
	Private Line
	Subway
	Monorail
	Stations
	Water

N

Odaiba Kaihin Park

Fuji TV
Headquarters

Ferris Wheel
Mega Web

Venus Fort

0 km   0.5   1   1.5   2 km

time flowing like a river

Such a huge and teeming metropolis, to see all of Tokyo at once a space-suit would be in order. Starting at the top of Tokyo Bay, the land officially under the jurisdiction of the Tokyo Metropolitan Government stretches far west into the mountains, and it even includes some small islands scattered to the south in the Pacific Ocean. Home to 12.5 million people, or 10 per cent of Japan's population, the territory is so vast that the head of Tokyo's government is given the title of governor rather than mayor.

The heart of Tokyo, however, consists of 23 wards that are centred on the Imperial Palace, near the bay. Even this area is large and complicated, with a population of 8.5 million people. Fortunately, geography and history break it down into two halves: the hilly west, and the watery east.

The Sumida River largely defines the older, eastern part of the city, and its flow from north to south in many ways retraces the flow of the city's history from past to future, with some of Tokyo's most traditional areas concentrated upstream and its most modern ones downstream.

Asakusa, one of the most visibly old-fashioned neighbourhoods, owes its very existence to the river. In the 7th century, nearly a millennium before Edo became the national capital, some fishermen were surprised to find a kannon bodhisattva statue mysteriously tangled in their nets. After their village chief enshrined this statue in his house, it became the nucleus of Senso-ji, also known as Asakusa Kannon Temple, which is the area's defining institution to this day.

The entrance to the temple grounds, called Kaminarimon (Thunder Gate), is a Tokyo landmark. Like many large Japanese temple gates, this one includes larger-than-life wooden statues of ferocious guardian deities on either side, each striking a dynamic pose that shows off their exaggerated muscular physiques. But as visitors walk between these guardians, they pass under the thing that makes Kaminarimon unique: a red paper lantern the size of a compact car.

PAGE 26: A businessman on the glowing walkway at Tokyo's International Forum.

THIS PAGE: The Rainbow Bridge affords some of the most exciting views in Tokyo.

OPPOSITE: Nakamise shopping street, the long main entryway to Senso-ji temple, is famous for its giant red lantern and multitudinous little shops.

While this gate sits on a busy city street, an even more crowded scene awaits within the temple grounds, as the stone path to the honden (main hall) is lined with stalls selling all manner of souvenirs. This has been the case since beyond living memory (British writer Isabella Bird noted the scene in her 1878 travelogue, *Unbeaten Tracks in Japan*), but an exploration of the surrounding area's side streets reveals numerous small merchants selling higher-quality goods in the form of handcrafted items ranging from ornate hair combs to Buddhist statuary.

One statue you're not likely to see, however, is the one fished out of the river all those years ago. If it still exists, it is sitting deep inside the dark interior of the massive honden, which casual visitors may not enter. The public is free to mount the steps leading to its high veranda, though, to toss some coins into a wooden trough and perhaps say a quick prayer. Many of the Buddhist faithful pause before a massive cauldron full of ashes and smouldering incense in the centre of the courtyard, add a few sticks of their own and then use cupped hands to sweep the fragrant smoke onto their bodies. Off to one side of the courtyard is a 55-m- (180-ft-) five-tiered pagoda, one of the tallest in Japan.

A few blocks west of Asakusa is Kappabashi, an area chock-a-block with restaurant supply stores. From sashimi knives to noodle pots to chopsticks by the pair or the hundred, it's all on display and for sale. A special category of item to watch for is the realistic plastic food that Japanese restaurants often put on display as a kind of 3D menu. The best of these ersatz edibles, deceptive in their realism, are custom-made, but it's possible to pick up some passable synthetic sushi on the spot.

ueno's collection of museums

Slightly further west is Ueno, another visibly old-fashioned area that harks back to a more recent century than Asakusa does. The neighbourhood centres on Ueno Park, which became the first public park in Tokyo when it opened in 1873. It has a very Western look that was typical of the Meiji period, with broad plazas, straight

THIS PAGE (FROM TOP): A humble monk holds out an alms bowl to people passing by; praying Buddhists use their hands to waft incense smoke onto themselves at Senso-ji.

OPPOSITE (FROM TOP): The Tokyo National Museum in Ueno Park holds the 2004, 2005 and 2006 records for the world's best-attended art exhibitions; contemporary art by Julian Opie at SCAI The Bathhouse.

walkways and showy fountains. The wide-open spaces account for this park being a magnet for spring cherry blossom viewing parties, but the crowds are so dense at that time of year that the atmosphere is more joyfully raucous than serenely contemplative.

Once the fleeting blossoms have fallen, attention turns to the park's more permanent attractions, such as the Tokyo Metropolitan Museum of Art, the National Science Museum and the Ueno Royal Museum. Outstanding art exhibitions, including collections of antiquities from around the world, frequently make stops here, but some of the museum buildings are worth a look in their own right. For instance, the International Library of Children's Literature is housed in a building dating back to 1906, but its 2002 refurbishment by world-renowned architect Tadao Ando adds a box-shaped glass entryway to the old stone building in a way reminiscent of IM Pei's glass pyramidal addition to the venerable stone buildings of the Louvre. Similarly, behind the Tokyo National Museum you will find the Gallery of Horyuji Treasures, built in 1999 to display Buddhist artworks from a temple in Nara. It was designed by Yoshio Taniguchi, who has since become better known for his Museum of Modern Art in New York. The National Museum of Western Art, built in 1959, is impossible to miss. This largely windowless stone block of a building can be appreciated either as a representative

work of its designer, Le Corbusier, or as a neutral backdrop for the museum's sculpture garden, where permanent features include Rodin's Thinker and his tall, imposing Gates of Hell. And just outside of Ueno Park to the northwest is SCAI The Bathhouse, a privately run contemporary art gallery in a graceful old building that was originally designed as—you guessed it—a bathhouse.

The artwork most associated with Ueno Park is the larger-than-life statue of Takamori Saigo, a 19th-century military leader who fought for, and then against, the new Meiji government. He died a rebel in 1877, was posthumously pardoned in 1891, and was memorialised in five tonnes of bronze in 1898. His chubby, smiling figure stands on a small promontory at the south end of the park, wearing windblown robes and leading a small dog on a leash. He looks less like a warrior from the past than an emblem of Japan's cute-oriented pop culture present, which may explain why the statue is the park's de facto mascot today.

big men: big stars

A more abstract sculpture is the gigantic golden object on top of the Philippe Starck-designed Asahi Breweries Head Office, across the Sumida River from Asakusa. Several times larger than a city bus, this elongated blob is meant to represent a blowing flame, but its shape often inspires less flattering, more scatological comparisons. Most Tokyoites seem to like it anyway, regarding it with a kind of wry affection.

Further proof that the city welcomes experimental designs may be found nearby at the northern terminus of the Tokyo Water Cruise service. The vessels cruising down the river to Tokyo Bay share the long, low lines of Paris' bateaux mouches, and for the same reason: there are many low bridges along the way. One of the boats, however, looks like nothing ever seen on the Seine. This is the 171-passenger vessel Himiko, designed by manga and anime artist Leiji Matsumoto. Its glowing floors and teardrop-shaped glass dome over the cockpit make it look like a cross between a spaceship and a living creature.

Slightly downstream is another startling work of design, the Edo-Tokyo Museum. Created by architect Kiyonori Kikutake and opened in 1993, this building holds several floors of historical exhibits, including life-size mock-ups of old streets. The entire structure, shaped like a flattened pyramid, is elevated three storeys above the ground by four massive pillars. Thanks to the pillars, the museum looms above the otherwise equally large Kokugikan sumo arena next door. More than just a showcase for Japan's biggest sports stars, sumo is also a Shinto ritual with roots dating back 1,500 years. Referees and judges still wear priestly regalia, and the wrestlers toss salt into the clay-floored ring as a gesture of purification before each bout. Sheltering the ring is a roof of a Shinto temple that hangs from the ceiling of this modern arena on cables, as if it were a jumbotron. Matches are held several times a year, and are sometimes attended by members of the imperial family.

Sumo's cultural roots inspire nationalist feelings, which long stood as a barrier to foreigners who wanted to step into the ring. But nowadays that has changed. American and Mongolian wrestlers have reached the sport's highest rank in recent years, and the handsome Bulgarian wrestler Kotooshu emerged as a national heartthrob.

Most sumo wrestlers carry a lot of fat on their large frames to reinforce their inertia and momentum. But that fat rides on top of even greater quantities of muscle. Wrestlers pack on both kinds of weight by eating copious helpings of chanko nabe, a hearty stew of meat, vegetables and seafood that is available at speciality restaurants that are often run by retired wrestlers. Try it just the once in order to remain svelte.

THIS PAGE (FROM TOP): *Though surrounded by pageantry, sumo bouts still take place in a simple ring of bare clay; a sumo wrestler bulks up with a bowl of chanko nabe stew.*

OPPOSITE (FROM LEFT): *Philippe Starck's golden ornament atop the Asahi Beer building; an avuncular statue of military leader Takamori Saigo.*

THIS PAGE (FROM TOP): Delicious and expensive red flesh lies beneath a layer of white frost on these solidly frozen tuna awaiting auction at the Tsukiji fish market; the dawn light on a sign.

OPPOSITE (FROM TOP): Blown-up blowfish can be used as both a decoration and food; sliced sashimi from master of Japanese cuisine Chef Murata.

In the winter, a wide variety of other nabe stew dishes appear at many other Tokyo restaurants. It's usually cooked in an earthenware pot right at the table, and ladling it out to friends is a great way to bring a dinner party to life. Japanese love participatory cuisine, with other examples including shabu-shabu and sukiyaki, which involve cooking thinly sliced meat in a bubbling pot of water or broth; okonomiyaki, in which diners flip patties of batter mixed with meat and vegetables on a griddle at their table; and yakiniku, in which everyone grills assorted slices of meat over glowing wooden charcoal amid fragrant smoke and lively chatter.

city of seafood

The platonic ideal of Japanese food is something much simpler: two pieces of tuna sushi placed side by side on a small earthenware dish or pale block of wood. This is the archetypal image of a cuisine renowned for its simple yet mysteriously elegant presentation of fresh, high-quality ingredients. The rich redness of the raw tuna contrasts with the pure whiteness of the rice, perhaps accented by a modest dab of green wasabi or a few shavings of pickled ginger off to one side. Visually appealing—and every bit as delicious as it looks—such a dish reduces its few ingredients to their most elemental forms, paradoxically heightening the diner's appreciation and enjoyment of them. A properly prepared plate of sushi is a textbook example of the Japanese aesthetic concept of wabi, which refers to finding beauty in simplicity and even austerity.

The Tsukiji fish market, also on the Sumida River, is one reason why there is so much good sushi to be had in Tokyo. Possessing a timeless feel, this bustling city within a city deals in about 450 different kinds seafood, from mussels to mackerel and squid to salmon. Most famous is its pre-dawn tuna auction, where rows of frozen fish weighing 100–200 kg (220–440 lbs) apiece lie on the ground in a shallow layer of undulating mist as buyers gather round. Bidding on the choicest specimens has reached as high as 100,000 yen per kilogram.

Virtually every edible species from the sea passes through Tsukiji's stalls, including exotic invertebrates that reward the adventurous eater. A couple to try are sea cucumber, which is sweet and colourful when marinated, and sea urchin, which is rich and buttery when raw. The truly daring can sample fugu, also known as blowfish. Certain parts of this fish contain a deadly poison, so it must be dissected and served with the greatest skill and care. Many fugu restaurants have display tanks facing the pavement, so passers-by can come eye to eye with these unearthly creatures, which are often the size of a large man's shoe. Blowfish also have a startling non-culinary use: inflated and shellacked, they can be turned into humorous-looking lanterns.

tokyo's master chefs

One place to be initiated into the ranks of fugu eaters is a restaurant called Nakajima in nearby Ginza. From November to March, chef Tadahiko Nakajima expertly prepares multi-course meals featuring fried fugu, fugu sashimi and fugu nabe stew. Year-round, his eponymous restaurant also serves a range of elegant kaiseki dishes. This style of Japanese haute cuisine reflects its tea ceremony roots through its refined flavours and exquisite visual presentation. (For more on kaiseki, see Beyond Tokyo.)

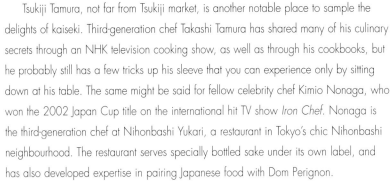

Tsukiji Tamura, not far from Tsukiji market, is another notable place to sample the delights of kaiseki. Third-generation chef Takashi Tamura has shared many of his culinary secrets through an NHK television cooking show, as well as through his cookbooks, but he probably still has a few tricks up his sleeve that you can experience only by sitting down at his table. The same might be said for fellow celebrity chef Kimio Nonaga, who won the 2002 Japan Cup title on the international hit TV show *Iron Chef*. Nonaga is the third-generation chef at Nihonbashi Yukari, a restaurant in Tokyo's chic Nihonbashi neighbourhood. The restaurant serves specially bottled sake under its own label, and has also developed expertise in pairing Japanese food with Dom Perignon.

One of the most exclusive restaurants located on the eastern side of Tokyo is Kanetanaka, which dates back to the Edo period. To dine at the main branch, in Ginza, you'll need to have made a firm reservation and have a deep appreciation of traditional Japanese culture. This is one of the few places in Tokyo in which real geisha still perform, meaning that guests—limited to the truest of connoisseurs—must be prepared for a night of refined entertainment as well as an elegant kaiseki meal. At a new branch of Kanetanaka in Shibuya's Cerulean Tower, on the west side of town, there's a special dining room offering slightly less rarefied entertainment: a view of the stage of an adjacent noh theatre.

THIS PAGE (FROM TOP): Coloured fluorescent lighting tubes are just one item for sale in Akihabara; a young Japanese couple enjoy Dance Dance Revolution, a game played with the feet.

OPPOSITE: Bright, shiny and noisy, pachinko parlours, where a kind of vertical pinball is played, are everywhere in Japan; the adored manga comic book.

akihabara: pixel paradise

"Japan is the global imagination's default setting for the future." So declared William Gibson, the best-selling science fiction novelist who is often credited with coining the term cyberspace. Gibson is clearly on to something, at least regarding Tokyo, which is fast on its way to becoming the first real-life city with more pixels than bricks.

Cyberspace and public space have certainly begun to merge in this digitised metropolis. Part of everyday life, television broadcasts are beamed directly to the screens of mobile phones, feature-length movies are available

for downloading to palmtop computers, touch-screen menus are now appearing in restaurants, and video monitors are being installed into the walls of a growing number of railway carriages. Anyone living in Japan who doesn't already own a digital TV is in the market for one: with all broadcasting in the nation switching over to that format in 2011, traditional analogue TVs will literally become obsolete.

Technological neophilia pervades Tokyo, but nowhere more than in Akihabara, a neighbourhood also known as Electric Town, located 1 km (½ mile) east of the Sumida River on its tributary the Kanda River. Large computer and electronics stores such as Laox, Sato Musen, T-Zone, Sofmap and more line Chuo-dori and its surrounding side streets, with some stores occupying several buildings. Even if you're not buying anything, this bustling district is a good place for people watching and taking in the atmosphere. There are dozens of smaller shops specialising in video games and their associated goods, such as character costumes and action figures, making Akihabara the epicentre of Tokyo's 'otaku' geek subculture.

Once looked down upon, otaku now enjoy increasingly positive mainstream attention. The geek-meets-chic pop culture phenomenon *Densha Otoko*, or *Train Man*, is a love story between an otaku and a fashionable woman (nicknamed Hermès, after the brand) whom he meets on a train that he boards at Akihabara Station. The purportedly true story became one of the top hits of the 2000s, turning into a book, a movie, a TV show and several different manga comic books.

marunouchi: dressed to make a killing

The Yamanote train line travels in a continuous oval that strings together most of Tokyo's major neighbourhoods like jewels on a necklace. Two stops south of the silicon pearl that is Akihabara comes the jumbo ruby of Tokyo Station itself. The east side of this landmark building is an ornate structure of red bricks and white stone, more than two city blocks wide and punctuated by three rotundas. The station opened in 1914 as a grand gateway to the Imperial Palace, located a few blocks east. Ornate cupolas originally topped its rotundas, but those were destroyed in World War II and were replaced with simpler peaked roofs. However, a restoration project now underway is due to return the east side of the station to its former glory in 2011.

The station has a staggering 28 platforms where 3,900 trains carrying 900,000 passengers stop each day. Some of that activity is underground, but much of it—including the graceful comings and goings of Shinkansen bullet trains—can be observed as a silent spectacle, from the windows of the Four Seasons Hotel Tokyo at Marunouchi. The whole scene is beautifully lit at night.

THIS PAGE: The redbrick Tokyo Station is a beloved monument to an earlier time.
OPPOSITE: The leafy streets of Marunouchi, the location of one of several dazzling Christmas illuminations around Tokyo.

The Marunouchi district also extends east of the station, where it is a forest of mostly brand-new skyscrapers that house the Tokyo headquarters of numerous banks and other businesses. Many of these buildings have attractive conservative stone façades on their lower floors—the better to harmonise with the red-brick ambience of the historic station—only to convert to a glassy, contemporary look higher up—the better to take advantage of the sunlight and views of the city.

The area from the centre of Marunouchi northward is home to several powerful media companies, including the Tokyo offices of Bloomberg and the world headquarters of *The Yomiuri Shimbun*, Japan's largest newspaper that has a daily circulation of more than 10 million. The paper's English version, *The Daily Yomiuri*, is one of three daily English-language newspapers published in Tokyo. Nearby are the offices of the *Nikkei*, Japan's equivalent of *The Wall Street Journal*. This newspaper's 'Nikkei average' is the standard measurement for tracking the fluctuations of the Tokyo Stock Market.

A decade ago, Marunouchi was strictly a buttoned-down business district. But the area immediately south of these media nerve centres has let its hair down recently and blossomed into one of Tokyo's major new centres of style as well. A central street, Marunouchi Naka-dori, has wide, tree-lined, pedestrian-friendly pavements that are adorned with an ever-changing array of large sculptures, and the whole neighbourhood has played host to whimsical outdoor Cow Parade exhibitions in which dozens of artists compete to create the most striking artwork based on a life-sized figure of a cow.

Naka-dori, about 10 blocks long, is full of chic, high-end clothing stores such as Emporio Armani, Kate Spade, Yves Saint Laurent, John Paul Gaultier, Charles Jourdan, Hermès and more. Japanese fashion house Takeo Kikuchi has a menswear shop called Fellas here, which pulls together the neighbourhood's various themes by dressing up-and-coming young tycoons in smart-looking business attire with a sharp new edge. There are also numerous shops specialising in luxury goods such as Tumi bags, Bottega Veneto leather goods, Facial Index eyewear and Baccarat crystal. Local Anglophiles are attracted to the Aquascutum and Harrods stores.

Francophiles find even more to love in Marunouchi, such as the patisserie of prize-winning chef Sadaharu Aoki, who opened two shops in Paris before coming home to set up another two in Tokyo. And then there's Les Caves Taillevent restaurant and wine shop, which caters to Tokyo's ever-growing thirst for the fruit of the vine. High above it all is Sens & Saveurs, a restaurant by the Michelin-starred twins Jacques and Laurent Pourcel. Located on the 35th floor of the Marunouchi Building, it has a view of the

THIS PAGE (FROM TOP): Dozens of small, boisterous watering holes are shoehorned beneath the railway tracks around Tokyo and Yurakucho stations; Artwork is projected onto the façade of the Mitsui Building.

OPPOSITE (FROM TOP): An artist sketches the Nihonbashi Bridge; the Chanel building features an ever-changing array of animated electronic images.

Imperial Palace. Also commanding impressive views from the same floor of the same building is the Thai restaurant Mango Tree. As a crowning touch, The Peninsula Tokyo is at the southern end of Marunouchi Naka-dori.

nihonbashi

Marunouchi may be Tokyo's newest shopping destination, but Nihonbashi, to the east of Tokyo Station, has a strong claim to being the oldest. A merchant named Takatoshi Mitsui operated a dry goods store here in the late 1600s, and the business has come down to the present day in the form of the Mitsukoshi department store. (Another of Mitsui's ventures was a corporate ancestor of the Sumitomo Mitsui Banking Corporation.)

Mitsukoshi's neighbours include the Bank of Japan—which issues currency and sets interest rates—and the luxurious Mandarin Oriental, Tokyo. The central bank runs a currency museum whose exhibits include a stone coin the size of a car tyre from the island of Yap, while the hotel offers sweeping views of the city from 38th-floor lobby windows that are roughly the size of tennis courts. But Nihonbashi was a prestigious part of town long before these parties came along. The neighbourhood takes its name, which literally means Japan Bridge, from a bridge built by the shogun Ieyasu Tokugawa in 1603, the first year of his rule. It was the official starting point of the national highway system, as shown by a small monument marking the zero milestone on the north shore of the Nihonbashi River, which, like the Kanda River, is a tributary of the Sumida.

There have been several different Nihonbashi bridges over the years, with an early arched, wooden variety serving as the scene for a 19th-century woodblock print by Hiroshige, the first picture in his famous *Tokaido Road* series. The current span, which may have been influenced by the Alexander III Bridge in Paris, dates to 1911. Supported by two stone arches, this bridge is decorated with ornate lamp-posts and bronze sculptures of lions and dragons. Unfortunately, a modern elevated highway passing overhead partially spoils the view.

glamorous ginza

A few blocks south of Nihonbashi you will find Tokyo's most famous shopping district—Ginza. Window-shopping is an art here; the window displays and buildings are part of the art themselves. The amazing flagship stores of several designer brands have made Ginza a showcase of cutting-edge architectural design. The Chanel store puts on a light show at night, mostly in the form of enormous graffiti-like writing

...amazing flagship stores of several designer brands have made Ginza a showcase of cutting-edge architectural design

that crawls up, down and sideways across the multi-storey façade. The Hermès store, designed by Renzo Piano in 2001, is a glowing tower of glass bricks, while the Mikimoto flagship, designed by Toyo Ito in 2005, looks like a 10-storey block of Swiss cheese. Architect Jun Aoki's Louis Vuitton building—one of many he has created for the brand—looks like a present wrapped in elegant checked paper. His protégé, architect Kumiko Inui, has wrapped the Christian Dior building in two floating layers of white steel, each stippled with holes and lit from behind.

Chic Ginza merchants proffer everything from pearls to paper. Major jeweller Tasaki has the pearls—not to mention diamonds and other gems—while famed stationer Ito-ya offers three adjacent buildings full of paper and related goods. Jewellery designers Shinji and Matico Naoi have their own shop, Atelier Shinji, in the area, too.

The most recognisable face of Ginza for most Tokyoites is the landmark clock tower and bowed stone façade of the Wako building at the corner of Harumi-dori and Chuo-dori, the area's central and very busy intersection. Destroyed in the 1923 earthquake, it was rebuilt in 1932, and is one of the few buildings to have survived World War II. A few blocks southeast on Harumi-dori stands the Kabuki-za theatre, home to an even more traditional aspect of the neighbourhood.

There's nothing to top off a day of shopping or theatre-going like a good meal. In addition to the venerable Japanese restaurants in the area, Il Pinolo is well-regarded for its Italian dishes. And if you're the type who skips straight to dessert, Il Pinolo also runs a cake shop in the basement of Ginza's Mitsukoshi department store. Chef Sam Leong's interpretation of Singaporean-Chinese cooking can be sampled at My Humble House, part of the Singapore-based Tung Lok Group, while the Sky restaurant, emphasising its organic ingredients, aims to present dishes that are as nourishing as they are enticing.

French cuisine is always a popular choice for a special night out, and Ginza offers plenty in that regard, too. Shiseido, a leading Japanese cosmetics firm, brought the elegant French restaurant L'Osier into being in Ginza many years ago. It seems personal beauty or high fashion and fine food go hand in hand in Tokyo; a similar

THIS PAGE (FROM TOP): *A doorman duly awaits customers at the gleaming Dior store; a Ginza shopper heads home.* OPPOSITE: *The cylindrical San-Ai building and the Wako clock tower, two Ginza landmarks, bracket the neighbourhood's main intersection.*

connection is that of world-renowned celebrity chef Alain Ducasse, who is the creator of Beige, a restaurant in the previously mentioned Chanel building. Also along the lines of beauty, the Ginza restaurant Le 6eme Sens d'Oenon orchestrates its guests' experience under the concept of using a sixth sense to enjoy wine and art.

toasting tokyo

Tokyo is a city that loves to drink. Sake, cocktails, beer and wine flow in abundance, and yet the city somehow maintains its imperturbable air of civilisation. If one does have a few too many during a night out, in a unique Japanese style, nothing will be said about it the next day. The smooth surface of life is quickly restored.

No one should ever leave Tokyo without trying at least a sip of sake, one of Japan's best-known contributions to world Epicureanism. One sip of this smooth, subtle and potent rice-based beverage is likely to lead to another. Sake can be served at almost any temperature, with hot sake being a favourite winter treat. Usually sipped from thimble-like ceramic cups, sake can also be enjoyed from a boxlike wooden container called a masu. Some bars serve sake in a tall glass standing inside a masu, with both filled to the brim.

Sake comes in countless varieties, as evidenced by the popularity of jizake, or local sakes. There are hundreds of different jizakes from around the nation, and connoisseurs find great satisfaction in exploring how the local spring water, the regional rice crop or the specific production methods impart subtle differences to each type. A good place to start your own sake-tasting adventure would be Fukumitsuya, with its main Tokyo branch in Ginza.

Awamori is a speciality of Okinawa, in the far south of Japan, that can be enjoyed in many bars and restaurants around Tokyo. In contrast to sake's brewed beginnings, awamori is a distilled rice beverage. Strong and exceptionally smooth, it is best sipped straight, on the rocks. Shochu, another distilled beverage, is usually made from sweet potatoes, but can also be produced using rice, buckwheat or brown sugar. In Tokyo,

THIS PAGE (FROM TOP): Chef Alain Ducasse with two of his staff from the Beige restaurant; a table setting at Beige.
OPPOSITE (FROM TOP): Clean lines and pale earth tones at the Fukumitsuya sake bar; a kimono-clad waitress hefts a jumbo bottle of sake.

one will often find it as the base of Japanese cocktails whose names end with the word hai. An oolong-hai, for instance, is iced oolong tea with shochu, while a ringo-hai is apple juice with shochu. At many bars and restaurants, patrons ordering a grapefruit-hai, a drink especially popular among young women, will be served a fresh grapefruit along with a juicer. The drinker then squeezes her own grapefruit juice as desired into a waiting glass of shochu.

Surprisingly, the average person in most parts of Japan rarely touches wine. But you'd never guess that on a visit to Tokyo, though, where wine drinking is widespread and quite chic. There are fine wine shops throughout the city, wine-tasting events occur fairly often, and top hotels and restaurants often have a professional sommelier on their staff. In fact, a Japanese named Shinya Tasaki was crowned as the top sommelier in the world in a 1995 competition, and he is still hailed as a celebrity in Tokyo. So familiar with European wines has this city become that the arrival of the Beaujolais Nouveau is now as reliable a sign of the coming of autumn as the changing colours of the leaves. Eleven million bottles of it were ordered in Japan in 2006.

Whichever drink takes your fancy, alcohol is a part of daily life in Tokyo and indeed the whole of Japan. From festivals to after-work drinks, a resonating kampai! (cheers!) can be heard throughout the year.

the future begins at shiodome

Just south of Ginza, and right on the banks of the Sumida River, is a neighbourhood few have ever seen, unless their last visit to Tokyo was during a year beginning with '2'. Shiodome is a sci-fi forest of skyscrapers, nearly all of them built in the infancy of the 21st century. In the late 1990s, the ground in most of this area was bare and flat, but now it is sometimes hard to be sure exactly where ground level is. Spacious plazas spread across the bottoms of deep, canyon-esque courtyards, with street-level traffic passing by two or three storeys overhead on one side while shining towers of glass and steel soar dozens of storeys higher on the other. In one such man-made valley, massive decorative columns that are softly illuminated from within at night actually rise past street level—but not quite as high as the extensive latticework of elevated sidewalks that knits the area together for pedestrians. Higher still are the elevated tracks of the Yurikamome, a fully automated train that takes hundreds of passengers to and fro with no human engineer or conductor aboard. To get some true perspective on Shiodome, an even

THIS PAGE: The expression 'ugo no takenoko' (bamboo shoots after rain) captures a sense of the sudden sprouting of sleek skyscrapers in Shiodome.

OPPOSITE: Gordon Ramsay's brasserie Cerise at the Conrad Tokyo offers breakfast, lunch and dinner every day of the week.

loftier vantage point is necessary, such as a table at the Oregon Bar and Grill, on the 42nd floor of the Shiodome City Center Building. For slightly less vertiginous vistas, try the 28th-floor French restaurant run by Scottish celebrity chef and former professional football player, Gordon Ramsay, inside the Conrad Tokyo Hotel. In addition to the eponymous Gordon Ramsay at Conrad Tokyo, the hotel is also home to his Cerise brasserie. The hotel occupies the 28th–37th floors of the Tokyo Shiodome Building, right next to the Yurikamome's Shiodome Station. On the opposite side of the station stands Shiodome Media Tower, in which the Park Hotel Tokyo is located.

Other buildings in this area house the Dentsu Shiki Theatre, the Shiodome Museum, and various corporate offices including the headquarters of the Nippon Television network. In a nod to the past, there is also a reconstruction of the original 19th-century Shimbashi railway station, now called 'Old Shimbashi Station' to distinguish it from the active Shimbashi Station nearby. A small, handsome building made of stone that was the pride of Meiji period Tokyo, it could easily have seemed out of place in this ultra-modern neighbourhood. Fortunately, it is given just enough room to breathe, and it stands as an elegant counterpoint to the futuristic towers that surround it.

Another vestige of bygone times is the Hamarikyu Gardens, a watery landscape where shoguns once enjoyed duck hunting. This is the point on the Sumida River where old Tokyo finally ends, and futuristic Tokyo firmly takes over. Looking downriver beyond the garden, the view is dominated by the spectacular Rainbow Bridge. Built in 1993, this 1.5-km- (1 mile-) suspension bridge has a central span of 570 m (1,870 ft), and its two towers rise 120 m (400 ft) above the water, equivalent to the height of a 40-storey building. The unmanned Yurikamome trains, plus view-seeking pedestrians and a great deal of highway traffic, cross this bridge in a steady stream, connecting downtown Tokyo to a string of newly developed bay-side areas that begins with Odaiba.

odaiba: consumer playland

In the days before the Rainbow Bridge was built, much of Odaiba consisted of windswept vacant lots. There's still plenty of open space here, but now it is much more carefully landscaped, and it is broken up by a number of large buildings that stand as examples of the shopping mall renaissance Japan has undergone in recent years. Not only are new malls opening up one after another in Tokyo and other major cities in Japan, but they are often designed as both shopping and entertainment centres. Odaiba is home to several of them.

The mall nearest the bridge is Decks, which includes the Sega Joypolis virtual reality amusement park. Inside, theatres with moving seats and surrounding video screens simulate experiences ranging from white water rafting trips to encounters with dinosaurs.

BELOW: A replica of the Statue of Liberty stands near the beach at Odaiba, with central Tokyo and the Rainbow Bridge behind her.

Out in the mall, even the shopping areas continue the amusement-park theme, with one part of Decks modelled to resemble the narrow, winding streets of old Hong Kong and another area made up like 1950s Tokyo—or at least someone's imaginary versions of those two bygone places. The Aqua City mall next door is a bit more conventional, if one overlooks the replica of the Statue of Liberty standing at the water's edge outside it. Restaurants in both malls enjoy stunning views of a small cove where lantern-lit takarabune pleasure boats gather in the evenings, with the Rainbow Bridge and Tokyo skyline lighting up beyond.

The Mori Building company is responsible for several of Tokyo's highest-profile modern landmarks, and it has made its mark on Odaiba, too, with the Venus Fort shopping mall. Designed as a 'retail and leisure theme park for women', it has 154

outlets that focus mainly on fashion, cosmetics and accessories. There is a complete range of stores including luxury brands and small boutiques. The building itself is remarkable in that the interior shopping corridors resemble a Baroque European streetscape, complete with statuary-filled fountains at the 'plazas' where halls intersect. The ceiling is a blue trompe l'oeil sky dotted with puffy white clouds artfully lit so that it shifts from dawn to noon to dusk several times in the course of a natural day.

Less glamorous, and perhaps more for men, is Toyota's Mega Web complex adjacent to Venus Fort. The Mega Web successfully turns shopping for cars into a form of entertainment, even for the least likely of car-lovers. In addition to displaying all of the company's latest models, the Mega Web also allows visitors to drive prototype electric vehicles around an enclosed track, tour a museum of classic cars and concept cars, or even go for a ride in a Joypolis-style racing car simulator.

Towering over the Toyota complex is a staggeringly huge Ferris wheel that, at 110 m (360 ft) in diameter and 115 m (377 ft) in total height, briefly held the title of world's biggest. Its 64 gondolas include two that are wheelchair-accessible and eight that have transparent floors. A full revolution takes 16 minutes, providing a silent respite from the crowds below. Even more impressive than the views from the top, though, are views of the wheel seen from a distance at night. Its nearly 10,000 sq-m- (107,600 sq-ft-) surface is the canvas for an amazing light show that is the most startling feature of Tokyo's skyline, with multicoloured patterns resembling Catherine wheels, flowers, bull's-eyes and windmills.

By day, though, the most striking landmark in Odaiba is the Kenzo Tange-designed Fuji Television headquarters building. It's actually a pair of 25-storey buildings connected by several flying walkways that support a six-storey sphere floating in the space between. This ingenious design was meant to evoke the giant eye that is the TV network's logo. On the upper floors of the globe, the observation deck offers views of the city and, very rarely, views of Mount Fuji.

The Odaiba-led shopping mall renaissance has spread across Japan, but the latest manifestation of it is right in the adjacent neighbourhood, Toyosu, where an amusement-shopping mall called Lalaport Toyosu, officially nicknamed 'Urban Dock,' opened in late 2006. Built to visually suggest a dockside warehouse being served by several ships (which are actually part of the building), the mall is home to an indoor park called Kidzania. Here, children can enter a mini town and try their hand at various grown-up jobs ranging from fire-fighters to bank clerks.

dancing to disney

Tokyo's bay-side areas also offer a few forms of entertainment that are not directly related to shopping, one of which is dancing. The majority of Tokyo's major nightclubs are on the west side of the city, in the hills, but one of the very best stands all by itself at the water's edge in an area called Shinkiba, just east of Odaiba.

This is Ageha, where some of the world's highest-paid international DJs come to play. Junior Vasquez, for instance, is among those who have actually gone so far as to mix an album at this club. Despite its undeniably powerful cachet, Ageha is a bit off the beaten path from a Tokyo nightlife point of view, so the management sometimes runs buses to Shibuya through the night, maintaining a vital logistical link to the generally cooler west side of town.

But when the temperatures change in the summer, the bay-side area becomes the hotter place, as the Chiba Marine Stadium in Makuhari, Chiba Prefecture (technically just outside of Tokyo), plays host to the Summer Sonic music festival. Begun in 2000,

THIS PAGE (FROM TOP): *Young Japanese women share a drink at an all-night music club; a well-stocked bar to keep the party aloft.*

OPPOSITE: *The cyclopean spherical eye of the Fuji TV building affords its visitors a sweeping view of the city.*

Summer Sonic is a showcase for rock, punk and hip hop acts. Past headlining performers have been Muse, Daft Punk, Metallica and The Flaming Lips. The two-day, two-city event (Osaka shares it) drew a combined attendance of 166,000 in 2006.

Music fans in Tokyo are spoiled for choice when it comes to summer festivals, as Summer Sonic has to compete every year with the Fuji Rock Festival, held outdoors in the mountains west of Tokyo. That event attracted 115,000 participants over its three-day run in 2006, which featured the Red Hot Chili Peppers, Sonic Youth, Franz Ferdinand, The Strokes and Happy Mondays.

Another difficult choice awaits visitors to the Tokyo Disney Resort: would you rather visit Disneyland or DisneySea? When Tokyo Disneyland opened in 1983, it was the first Disneyland outside the US. When Tokyo DisneySea opened in 2001, it was the first DisneySea anywhere on earth. The two parks, standing side by side on the bay shore in Urayasu, Chiba Prefecture, just a few hundred metres outside Tokyo's official borders, draw a combined attendance of about 12 million people a year.

Both parks have their appeal, with Disneyland offering traditional attractions such as Space Mountain, Cinderella's Castle and the Haunted Mansion. And then there's that venerable old ride that Johnny Depp has ensured no one will ever see the same way again, the Pirates of the Caribbean.

DisneySea has a lagoon in its centre instead of a castle, and the surrounding 'lands' are based on watery themes, such as Mediterranean Harbor, American Waterfront, Arabian Coast and Mysterious Island. DisneySea is sometimes described as the more adult park because its sit-down restaurants serve wine and beer. Even in Mermaid Lagoon, the most seemingly kiddies-oriented part of DisneySea, there is a theatre with a live show that dazzles adults, with actors suspended in mid-air in elaborate fish costumes reminiscent of the animal outfits worn in the stage version of Disney's *The Lion King*.

Whichever park, Disney has managed to latch on to Japan's spirit for all things kawaii (cute), ensuring they remain a resounding success for a long while to come.

THIS PAGE (FROM TOP): Sound and light converge at the Summer Sonic music festival; DisneySea features a whale big enough to swallow a gift shop.

OPPOSITE: Twenty-four hour party people, grinning all night long, the 'peace' sign is a common greeting-cum-photo-pose among Japanese youth.

...Disney has managed to latch on to Japan's spirit for all things kawaii...

Conrad Tokyo

A breathtaking centrepiece—a red sculpture that dazzles against the dark, wooden-slatted walls—greets guests as they enter the hotel lobby. A fascinating blend of modern design and intricate Japanese style adorns every corner of the hotel to stunning effect.

Perched at the top of the Tokyo Shiodome Building, the Conrad has guestrooms that assume two distinct personalities. With panoramic views of the Hamarikyu Gardens, Rainbow Bridge and Tokyo Bay, the 'garden' rooms appear serene and exude a calming influence. Red

tones and lantern-style lamps in the 'city' rooms create an intimate setting, while their full-length windows offer a spectacular view of the surrounding skyscrapers. Each room is equipped with a giant plasma TV, DVD player and wireless phone. The bathrooms look sleek in their black granite and white

marble outfit, and a touch of class is added by the complimentary products designed exclusively for Conrad by Shiseido.

Outside, Shiodome is a modern retail and entertainment hub situated between Ginza and Tokyo's famous Hamarikyu Gardens—the bustling Tsukiji fish market nearby is a testament to the city's vibrancy.

Inside the quiet ambience of the hotel, Mizuki Spa provides the perfect contrast to the energy of the city outside. Combining Japanese design with Western-style service, the spa treatments provide an equally relaxing and rejuvenating experience. Inspired by the ancient form of Japanese painting, a sumie-style swimming pool complete with jet-black finishing that is encased in steel and glass makes it a dramatic setting for a spot of exercise.

Conrad is host to some of Tokyo's most dynamic restaurants, two of which are helmed by British celebrity chef Gordon Ramsay. Gordon Ramsay at Conrad Tokyo

and Cerise by Gordon Ramsay serve outstanding French cuisine. The 8-m- (26-ft-) walk-in wine cellar of China Blue is a masterpiece with its avant-garde décor; just as delectable is its Cantonese food. In Conrad's Japanese restaurant, black and white pillars form a spectacular contrast with vividly-coloured chairs. Offering kaiseki, teppanyaki and sushi with standard and tatami-style seating, Kazahana promises a stylish setting for guests to enjoy some excellent local cuisine.

FACTS		
ROOMS	290	
FOOD	Cerise by Gordon Ramsay: brasserie • China Blue: Chinese • Gordon Ramsay at Conrad Tokyo: modern French • Kazahana: Japanese	
DRINK	TwentyEight	
FEATURES	chapel • Mizuki Spa & Fitness • pool	
BUSINESS	business centre	
NEARBY	Ginza • Hamarikyu Gardens • Shiodome • Tsukiji Fish Market	
CONTACT	1-9-1 Higashi-Shinbashi, Minato-ku, Tokyo, 105-7337 • telephone: +81.3.6388 8000 • facsimile: +81.3.6388 8001 • email: tokyoinfo@conradhotels.com • website: www.conradhotels.com	

PHOTOGRAPHS COURTESY OF CONRAD TOKYO.

Four Seasons Hotel Tokyo at Marunouchi

Standing tall on Tokyo's busiest central business district is the prestigious Pacific Century Place. And occupying five storeys of this landmark glass tower is the Four Seasons Hotel Tokyo at Marunouchi, an idyllic sanctuary that forms the perfect contrast to the dynamism of Marunouchi. Upon entering the plush lobby, guests are not only struck by the unique blend of contemporary and traditional Japanese design of the interiors, but also by the hotel's personalised service and warm hospitality.

THIS PAGE (FROM TOP): *The luxurious bathrooms offer an equally spectacular view of the city; the Lobby Lounge and Bar serves a wide variety of drinks and snacks in a stylish setting.*

OPPOSITE (FROM LEFT): *Spacious guestrooms provide maximum comfort with a great city view; a deep-soaking tub in the bathroom ensures a most indulgent experience.*

While the showpiece open fireplace creates a warm and cosy feel, guests can also marvel at the exquisite objets d'art and artwork displayed throughout the hotel.

Taking advantage of the spectacular views are the floor-to-ceiling windows in the hotel's 57 spacious guestrooms. The minimalist yet tasteful design is very much in keeping with the Japanese philosophy of Zen, providing the ultimate retreat for comfort and relaxation. With state-of-the-art technology in every room, the guest is able to enjoy a wall-mounted 42-inch plasma TV, DVD player and Internet access.

For when hunger strikes, there is the Ekki Bar & Grill, which offers a sophisticated dining experience. There are only 66 seats

The hotel's elegant design combines seamlessly with its exclusive yet residential feel...

provides an excellent route. The spa is also a haven for a peaceful retreat, offering not only massages and rejuvenating treatments, but also the quintessential Japanese experience of the traditional onsen bath.

The Four Seasons Hotel Tokyo at Marunouchi is one luxury not to be missed. The hotel's elegant design combines seamlessly with its exclusive yet residential feel for a truly amazing experience, making it a real treat for both mind and body.

in the restaurant, meaning diners can enjoy an intimate setting in addition to the contemporary New York style cuisine prepared by a team of culinary experts. The hotel also provides function rooms for private occasions or company meetings.

For the health and fitness conscious, the 24-hour fitness studio offers a panoramic view of the city as well as the latest equipment for the ideal workout session. If jogging is preferred, the scenic 5-km- (3-mile-) trail at the nearby Imperial Palace

FACTS	
ROOMS	57
FOOD	Ekki Bar & Grill: international
DRINK	Lobby Lounge and Bar
FEATURES	24-hour fitness studio • Japanese hotspring bath • spa • steam room
BUSINESS	24-hour business centre • 2 meeting rooms • Internet • translation services
NEARBY	arts and culture • jogging • shopping
CONTACT	Pacific Century Place, 1-11-1 Marunouchi, Chiyoda-ku, Tokyo, 100-6277 • telephone: +81.3.5222 7222 • facsimile: +81.3.5222 1255 • email: reservations.mar@fourseasons.com • website: www.fourseasons.com

PHOTOGRAPHS COURTESY OF FOUR SEASONS HOTEL TOKYO AT MARUNOUCHI.

Mandarin Oriental, Tokyo

Originally the landmark of central Tokyo, Nihonbashi Bridge—the Bridge of Japan—has for centuries attracted shops, businesses, shrines and galleries to set up shop within its vicinity. Even as the bustling financial district continues to develop and grow around it, Nihonbashi firmly remains the historical and cultural heart of the city.

Occupying the top floors of the soaring Nihonbashi Misui Tower, Mandarin Oriental, Tokyo commands an astonishing view of the city. To the west, Mount Fuji cuts an impressive figure and provides a magnificent backdrop against the Imperial Palace Gardens on a clear day. To the southwest, the panoramic view that stretches across Tokyo Bay is breathtaking. Speeding up 38 floors in a private elevator and arriving at the hotel's spectacular glass lobby certainly ensures a dramatic and lasting first impression.

Well known for providing excellent service, comfort and innovative design, the Mandarin Oriental hotels rank among the best in the world. Here in Tokyo, their renowned attention to detail combines with the inspiring surroundings to create an exclusive six-star retreat. Throughout the hotel, delicate Japanese aesthetics, lavish ornaments and soft-glowing lanterns foster an aura of opulence mixed with Asian exoticism. Guestrooms—some of the city's biggest—are decorated with impressive artwork. An exclusive collection of isegata, the traditional stencil pattern for yukata (summer kimono) and now considered a valuable collector's item, hangs from the walls. Lanterns made of

THIS PAGE (CLOCKWISE FROM TOP):
Guests get to sample a wide range of refreshing teas at Sense Tea Corner; enjoy the breathtaking view of the city from the comfort of the luxurious guestroom; Signature mixes fine dining with an avant-garde décor.

OPPOSITE: Look forward to innovative Northern Italian cuisine in stylish Ventaglio.

washi, or Japanese paper, are suspended from the ceiling to the bedside table, ensuring adequate lighting for reading. Ever the thoughtful host, the hotel provides sleek-looking black lacquer boxes containing a souvenir traditional Japanese folding fan, as well as slippers and a kimono-style robe for guests to relax in. In the bathroom, guests can immerse themselves in an invigorating bath in three different showers—body, hand and rain—followed by a soak in the enormous stand-alone sunken bathtub.

Mandarin Oriental, Tokyo houses seven restaurants and bars that suit any mood or occasion. With seven of them sharing the dizzying heights of the top floors, they provide some of the city's most dazzling views as well. For style and sophistication, Signature offers French-inspired cuisine within its bustling open kitchen concept. Grey striped walls, stylised chairs and bold lighting set a modern-retro tone for the restaurant. Dramatic yet elegant, Sense serves contemporary Cantonese cuisine in a rich oriental setting with gold-stencilled ceilings and dark metal columns. Looking smart in their fuchsia pink outfits, waitresses add to the restaurant's overall style. For a nice cuppa after a meal, Sense Tea Corner is ideal. In a relaxed setting with more than 20 different fragrant teas from around the world to choose from, guests will enjoy themselves.

The Nihonbashi Misui Tower links directly to the city's subway stations for easy access to Narita Airport and sights within the city. Some of Tokyo's most popular attractions are also within easy walking distance, such as the Imperial Palace and the exclusive Ginza shopping hub. If there is no time for browsing in the nearby designer boutiques or the traditional, family-run shops, Mandarin Oriental, Tokyo has its own in-room shopping service. From a 28-page catalogue, guests can order anything from cotton duvet covers to high-precision telescopes along with traditional Japanese crafts and pottery.

PHOTOGRAPHS COURTESY OF MANDARIN ORIENTAL, TOKYO.

FACTS		
ROOMS	179	
FOOD	K'shiki: continental • Signature: French • Sense: Cantonese • Ventaglio: Italian • Oriental Lounge: afternoon tea and cocktails • Tapas Molecular Bar: Molecular cuisine • Mandarin Oriental Gourmet Shop	
DRINK	Mandarin Bar • Sense Tea Corner	
FEATURES	ballroom • meeting rooms • spa • wedding chapel • gym	
NEARBY	Ginza • Imperial Palace • Nihonbashi Bridge • Tokyo Central Station	
CONTACT	2-1-1 Nihonbashi-Muromachi, Chuo-ku, Tokyo, 103-8328 • telephone: +81.3.3270 8800 • facsimile: +81.3.3270 8828 • email: motyo-reservations@mohg.com • website: www.mandarinoriental.com/tokyo	

Park Hotel Tokyo

THIS PAGE (FROM TOP): *Decorated with Monique Le Houelleur's natural artwork and coloured with soothing tones, the Park Suite offers maximum comfort; Lofty original pillows aside, the hotel also provides professional advice on how to get a better night's sleep.*

OPPOSITE (FROM LEFT): *Eat healthily and enjoy the sophisticated setting of gastronomie française tateru yoshino; the magnificent atrium in the hotel lobby.*

Close to the shopping and entertainment district of Ginza, glimmering skyscrapers mark the centre of Tokyo's glamorous 'Media City', Shiodome, the commercial heart of the city. Occupying the top 10 floors of the Shiodome Media Tower with Shiodome Station right at its doorstep and Shimbashi within easy walking distance on the JR line, Park Hotel Tokyo sits in an enviably central position. With this in mind, the hotel offers a series of unique but brilliant accommodation schemes. Business travellers have the flexibility of making their reservations after the standard time at a discounted rate, while there are packages for guests interested in health and wellness programmes.

...guestrooms are comfortable and provide a calming touch...

Distinguished for its innovative style, Park Hotel Tokyo is an affiliate of the Design Hotels group, which recognises hotels for their original architectural design. Located on the 25th floor, the hotel reception is dominated by an impressive atrium that rises 10 floors up to a magnificent, hexagonal glass roof.

Decorated with famous French sculptor Monique Le Houelleur's artwork, guestrooms are comfortable and provide a calming touch with full-sized windows that offer a

sweeping view of the city. With trained pillow fitters to adjust the height of guests' pillows, such attention to detail ensures an enjoyable stay at the hotel. Guests can also request quick massages in the comfort and privacy of their own rooms, or receive full treatment at the hotel's Institut de Phyto-Aromatherapie. With over 30 essential oils blended to suit personal needs, it can be the perfect wind-down to the end of a busy day.

Combining award-winning designs with their commitment to health and well-being, the hotel's two restaurants, gastronomie française tateru yoshino and Hanasanshou, offer healthy, organic food in a modern setting. With his Michelin-starred restaurant, Stella Maris, Tateru Yoshino brings an original and home-style flair to the kitchens of gastronomie française. Over at Hanasanhou, diners will appreciate the cosy atmosphere and enjoy the traditional Kyoto cuisine while looking out at the star-studded skyline of Tokyo.

FACTS	**ROOMS**	273
	FOOD	Dining Bar • gastronomie française tateru yoshino: French • Hanasanshou: Japanese • News Art Café • Salon Chinois: Chinese • Salon Christolfe: Chinese, French and Japanese
	DRINK	bar à vins tateru yoshino • The Lounge
	FEATURES	affiliate of the Design Hotels group • business centre • Constance Spry Flower School and Shop • Institut de Phyto-Aromatherapie
	NEARBY	Ginza • Shimbashi
	CONTACT	Shiodome Media Tower, 1-7-1 Higashi-Shimbashi, Minato-ku, Tokyo, 105-7227 • telephone: +81.3.6252 1111 • facsimile: +81.3.6252 1001 • email: info@parkhoteltokyo.com • website: www.parkhoteltokyo.com

PHOTOGRAPHS COURTESY OF PARK HOTEL TOKYO.

The Peninsula Tokyo

With its superb location in the prominent business district of Marunouchi, The Peninsula Tokyo overlooks some of the city's most notable landmarks, including the Imperial Palace and the prestigious shopping district of Ginza. A short walk, or a luxurious ride in the hotel's immaculately restored 1934 Rolls-Royce Phantom will take guests down the designer streets of Ginza where internationally renowned shopping brands can be found. Directly connected to the Hibiya Station, the hotel is located right at the heart of Tokyo's sprawling underground metro system, making it an ideal base to explore the rest of the city.

In an intriguing mix, the hotel's modern setting emanates a distinct style of Japanese heritage and culture with the beautiful sliding camphor tree doors and elegant lacquer storage boxes that are on display. Guestrooms are contemporary and lavishly designed. The walk-in dressing room and huge marble bathroom will catch the eye, in addition to the separate living area with a breakfast table and work desk, creating a grand retreat in a bustling city. The commanding views of the Imperial Palace and the magnificent skyline of Shinjuku are just some of the perks guests can enjoy at the hotel. The range of facilities is excellent as

THIS PAGE (FROM TOP): Magnificent city views aside, The Peninsula Tokyo offers superb facilities as well as excellent service; guests will be impressed by the stylish interior and cosy ambience of the deluxe rooms.

OPPOSITE (FROM LEFT): Enjoy the luxury of the hotel's spacious walk-in dressing room; the marble bathroom provides maximum indulgence with its space, mood lighting and a separate bath and rain shower among other amenities.

...overlooks some of the city's notable landmarks, including the Imperial Palace...

From the famous Peninsula Afternoon Tea at The Lobby to Kyoto-style kaiseki delicacies at Tsuruya, the hotel offers a diverse range of culinary experiences. Designed in the style of a Suzhou garden, Hei Fung Terrace specialises in traditional Cantonese cuisine. At the Rooftop Restaurant and Bar, the extensive wine list and international menu are enhanced by an uninterrupted view of the city. For guests with a sweet tooth, The Peninsula Boutique & Café will satisfy cravings. Apart from its famous chocolates, the café also offers delicious pastries and premium coffees and teas. Paying tribute to its history, The Seven Seas Pacific Aviation Lounge covers a fascinating 100 years of civil aviation progress in Japan and also doubles up as a unique setting for private functions.

Drawing on Eastern and Western wellness and relaxation philosophies to re-balance both mind and body, the treatments at The Peninsula Spa by ESPA will ensure a rejuvenating start, or soothing wind-down to the day. Their signature treatment, Freedom of Life, is an Oriental dance body treatment. This powerful massage that includes body stretching, polarity balancing, a foot bath, body scrub, facial and head massage, will go a long way in clearing any strain and fatigue brought about by Tokyo's frenetic lifestyle.

they cater to both business and leisure travellers. Each room is fitted with a plasma TV and complimentary wireless Internet access among other impressive technological gadgets. An espresso machine and even a nail dryer are provided as well, ensuring top class service for everyone. Guests can also choose to relax by the pool or work out in the hotel's gym.

FACTS

ROOMS	314
FOOD	Hei Fung Terrace: Cantonese • Peninsula Boutique & Café: patisserie • Rooftop Restaurant and Bar: international • The Lobby: continental • Tsuruya: Japanese
DRINK	Rooftop Restaurant and Bar • The Lobby
FEATURES	fitness centre • pool • Rolls-Royce service• The Peninsula Spa by ESPA
NEARBY	Ginza • Hibiya Station • Hibiya Park • Imperial Palace • Marunouchi • Otemachi • Yurakucho
CONTACT	1-8-1 Yurakucho, Chiyoda-ku, Tokyo, 100-0006 • telephone: +81.3.6270 2888 • facsimile: +81.3.6270 2000 • email: ptk@peninsula.com • website: www.peninsula.com/tokyo

PHOTOGRAPHS COURTESY OF THE PENINSULA TOKYO.

Beige Alain Ducasse Tokyo

Boldness, perfection, passion and avant-garde. These are the qualities that embody the style of Beige Tokyo. With an award-winning menu, elegant décor and a stunning view of the city, most visitors to this stylishly unique restaurant would agree. Created from the first joint venture between Alain Ducasse and Chanel Japon, Beige is the ultimate collaboration between fashion, design and food.

Designed by New York architect Peter Marino, the restaurant interior is a tapestry of soothing and soft textures. Borrowing tones from Chanel's palette, it is no surprise that beige is the dominant colour, accented by shades of brown and gold. Japanese glass screens, silk banquettes and soft egg-shaped chairs create a simple yet sleek appearance throughout the restaurant, while glass windows and mirrors reflect the restaurant's soft lighting. Stunning tableware is sourced from around the world, and includes lacquer trays made by traditional craftsmen from Japan, tableware created by Israeli designer Ron Arad for Alessi, and martini glasses inspired by Alain Ducasse himself.

THIS PAGE (FROM TOP): The Chanel Tower, with its impressive glass façade, is home to Beige Tokyo; flair and elegance are evident in the restaurant's stylish décor.

OPPOSITE (FROM LEFT): The restaurant's cosy lounge is perfect for an after meal drink; with the captivating city nightlife in full view, dinner at Beige will leave guests with an unforgettable experience.

...mixes French culinary excellence with top quality ingredients.

Situated on the top floor of the Chanel Tower in Ginza, each table at Beige offers a spectacular view across the busy streets of Tokyo's most prestigious shopping district and beyond. Filled with shoppers and businessmen at lunchtime, and Tokyo's cosmopolitan crowd in the evenings, the buzz within the restaurant is as vibrant as the dazzling lights and weaving traffic below.

Surrounded by some of the world's most renowned produce, from Kobe beef to amadai—a salt water fish similar to sea bream found in the Yamaguchi region of Japan—Alain Ducasse mixes French culinary

excellence with top quality ingredients. Alongside à la carte options, the menu offers a formulaic guide for guests to design their own meals. In choosing dishes from a series of food categories such as vegetables, meat and fish, and foie gras, guests get to combine their selections with the chef's recommendations for one gastronomic meal. Specialities include Foie Gras Chestnut Flour Ravioli with Sautéed Vegetables and Duck Bouillon, Lobster from Brittany with Pearl Onions, Pumpkin Gnocchi and 'Civet' Sauce, and a Roasted Rack of Lamb with Melting Eggplants, Black Olives and Rosemary Juice.

A wine cellar as impressive as Alain Ducasse's remarkable menu is unsurprisingly French. With a great variety and different accents from the Bourgogne, Rhone and Bordeaux regions, the extensive Chanel list also offers exclusive vintages of Chateau Canon and Rauzan Segla, both owned by the Chanel Group.

FACTS

SEATS	86
FOOD	modern French
DRINK	lounge
FEATURES	extensive wine list • reservations up to 3 months in advance • spectacular views • wine cellar
NEARBY	Ginza • Shimbashi
CONTACT	10F Chanel Ginza Building, 3-5-3 Ginza, Chuo-ko, Tokyo 104-0061 • telephone: +81.3.5159 5500 • facsimile: +81.3.5159 5501 • email: info@beige.co.jp • website: www.beige-tokyo.com

PHOTOGRAPHS COURTESY OF BEIGE ALAIN DUCASSE TOKYO.

Il Pinolo at Ginza

With dark wooden flooring and tables forming the perfect contrast with its pristine white walls, the stylishly modern Il Pinolo first opened its doors in 2001. The restaurant's avant-garde interior complements well with its warm ambience, which is enhanced by the flickering candles and the small spotlights that light up the tables. Il Pinolo's location in Ginza's Chuo-dori places the Italian restaurant right at the heart of the sophisticated and upmarket shopping district of Ginza. Meaning 'pine nut', Il Pinolo serves a unique blend of traditional Tuscan cuisine with the special seasonal ingredients of Japan.

Traditional Tuscan taste focuses on the simplicity of dishes, where ingredients of each of the four seasons are harvested from the blessed terrain and mixed with

THIS PAGE (CLOCKWISE FROM TOP): Il Pinolo offers fine dining in a stylish and elegant setting; guests will enjoy the restaurant's exclusive yet cosy surroundings; sample the best of both worlds with Tuscan fare that is infused with local flavours.

OPPOSITE (FROM LEFT): Candles and soft lighting add to the restaurant's warm atmosphere; at Il Pinolo, wine tasting is very much on the agenda; a superb range of wines and after dinner liqueurs awaits the wine connoisseur.

an abundant portion of herbs. At Il Pinolo, this traditional flavour forms the base of each dish to which fresh ingredients are added to create an exceptional yet tantalising menu.

For the executive chef Kosaka, it has become a personal pastime to head out to the mountains and seas to personally source for and select the finest ingredients

...unique blend of traditional Tuscan cuisine with the special seasonal ingredients of Japan.

for his dishes. As proof of this kodawari principle, or uncompromising attention to detail, the producers of each ingredient are carefully selected to maintain the best quality. Guests will also find on the menu an excellent mélange of savoury Italian and Japanese specialities that includes Chestnut Garganelli Pasta with Satsuma Chicken, Chestnut Ragout and Foie Gras, and Roasted Kagoshima Pork with Organic Vegetables. For those with a sweet tooth, desserts such as the White Chocolate

Pudding accented with Truffle will tempt their taste buds, along with perennial favourites like tiramisu and gelato. A range of food courses is available, including a special degustation course for guests who wish to sample a variety of dishes from the menu, which changes seasonally.

Excellent food goes hand in hand with great wine, of which Il Pinolo keeps a daily stock of 180 different types on its extensive wine list. Indeed, wine lovers will be very pleased to find the rare Super Toscana

on the list. Guests get to taste up to eight different kinds of wines by the glass, which is one of the reasons why they always return to the establishment for more Il Pinolo-style fine dining. In fact, a wide range of after dinner liqueurs is also on offer, including the equally rare grappa.

With superb Italian cuisine and the finest wines available, Il Pinolo offers fine dining at its best. Guests can certainly look forward to an unforgettable dining experience in an elegant setting.

FACTS		
SEATS	62	
FOOD	Italian	
DRINK	wine list	
FEATURES	recommended wines • rare after dinner drinks • private dining rooms • spectacular night view	
NEARBY	Ginza • Margo Bar	
CONTACT	9F Ginza Green, 7-8-7 Ginza, Chuo-ku, Tokyo, 104-0061• telephone: +81.3.5537 0474 • facsimile: +81.3.5537 0475 • email: ilpinolo2@stillfoods.com • website: www.il-pinolo.com	

PHOTOGRAPHS COURTESY OF STILLFOODS INC.

L'Osier

What defines a fine French restaurant? Exceptional food, impeccable service and an excellent ambience are what most gourmets would agree on. This description fits the bill of many French establishments in Tokyo, but at L'Osier, the dining experience extends well beyond this.

Founded in 1973, L'Osier has steadily risen to the upper echelons of fine dining over the years. Today, this outstanding restaurant is located next to Shiseido's headquarters, which is right at the heart of the luxurious shopping region of Ginza. Like its posh surroundings in the renowned district of Ginza's Namiki-dori, L'Osier exudes an air of elegance that can be attributed to its partnership with Shiseido. With a belief in style and class, the restaurant espouses a spirit of art de vivre a la française, or French art of living.

Now headed by the executive chef Bruno Menard, L'Osier continues to satisfy every palate with renewed freshness.

THIS PAGE (CLOCKWISE FROM TOP): With more than 20 years of experience working in some of the world's top restaurants, Chef Menard has developed his own distinct menu; L'Osier offers an intriguing mix of tradition and modernism; sample the best of French cuisine in a stylish setting.
OPPOSITE: Excellent food and tantalising desserts cap an unforgettable dining experience at L'Osier.

Menard defines his 'neo-classic' cuisine as refined yet innovative and influenced by his experiences of living abroad. Indeed, Menard was the former head chef at The Dining Room—Atlanta Ritz Carlton's five-star restaurant—and also opened La Baie at The Ritz-Carlton, Osaka. In selecting the finest ingredients for his dishes, Menard ensures only the best are served. As testament to the restaurant's excellent food, L'Osier is usually fully booked for both lunch and dinner all year round; guests are recommended to make reservations to avoid disappointment.

Infusing the old with the new, Chef Menard prepares his dishes in the traditional way while applying new culinary methods for an even better taste. Above all, Menard wishes to prepare food that can be enjoyed and appreciated in every sense—a dish that is attractive, and just as delicious. 'La cuisine est ma vie', or 'cuisine is my life', is a value that Menard cherishes.

One of the chef's signature dishes is the Foie Gras Poêlée, which is topped with Argan Oil and a Mélange of Almonds and Ginger Confit. Even with unusual courses such as wild game, Menard's superb culinary skills mean guests get to taste the finest dishes. Remember to sample L'Osier's wide range of wines and savour its creatively prepared chocolate desserts, which are pleasantly light and the perfect way to round off a satisfying French meal.

At L'Osier, haute cuisine is served by the most attentive staff, ensuring a pleasant dining experience for all. For a touch of petit France in central Tokyo, L'Osier, which promises to be more than just excellent food, is one French restaurant not to be missed.

FACTS

SEATS	40
FOOD	French
DRINK	extensive wine list
FEATURES	private dining room
NEARBY	Ginza
CONTACT	7-5-5 Ginza, Chuo-ku, Tokyo, 104-8010 • telephone: +81.3.3571 6050 • facsimile: +81.3.3571 6080 • website: www.shiseido.co.jp/e/losier/index.htm

PHOTOGRAPHS COURTESY OF L'OSIER.

le 6eme sens d'OENON

It is said that food is best enjoyed when all five senses are triggered. The dining concept at le 6eme sens d'OENON is based on a gastronomic experience that strives to permeate the elusive sixth sense with its unique formula of food, wine, and art. The restaurant is located in the fashion district of Ginza and is managed by former sous-chef of the Tour d'Argent in Paris, Dominique Corby, who aims to extend his cooking beyond the five classic senses of sight, hearing, touch, smell and taste.

Firmly believing that food and wine go hand in hand, the original French dishes Corby makes combine traditional and creative tastes that complement any of the

THIS PAGE (FROM TOP): Chef Corby deep in concentration as he prepares one of his tantalising French dishes; with its soft orange glow, the dining room offers an exquisite yet cosy ambience.

OPPOSITE (FROM LEFT): The stylish glass façade at the entrance will attract anyone who walks past le 6eme sens d'OENON; a closer look at the restaurant's impressive wine collection.

10,000 bottles of wine in the restaurant's impressive wine cellar. Wine is a top priority here, and its spectacular collection should be no surprise. A manufacturer of Japanese sake, liqueur and shochu, Oenon is also an established Japanese fine wine distributor.

The entrance to le 6eme sens d'OENON is a grand glass façade that lines the retro-style corridor gai, or corridor street. Beyond this elegant frontage, an impressive glass display, showcasing the restaurant's tantalising wine collection, beckons the passer-by to walk in and savour a glass or two. Seating an intimate number of 24, guests are made to feel welcome in the cosy dining room that exudes a warm orange glow. With Cassina-designed chairs

a casual alternative, the café appears inviting with its casual bright orange chairs, and with its food prepared in the same kitchen as the restaurant's, the café's fare is just as delectable.

A fascinating mélange of an amazing gastronomic experience, a stellar collection of wine and an avant-garde interior ensures diners will certainly leave le 6eme sens d'OENON with their five senses—and sixth—very much satisfied.

and brightly decorated tabletops lit by the feathery chandeliers, diners will enjoy the restaurant's exclusive yet relaxing ambience.

There is stunning artwork such as the beautiful mosaics that decorate the walls. The various works of art and interior decoration are produced by the renowned Japanese engraving artist, Yoko Yamamoto.

Together, they make an evening at le 6eme sens d'OENON a feast for all senses. With a most indulgent dining experience guaranteed, a reservation is absolutely necessary to avoid disappointment. Four courses are offered for both lunch and dinner, while à la carte items can also be enjoyed at the café and bar area. Offering

FACTS

SEATS	63
FOOD	contemporary French
DRINK	champagne • cocktails • digestifs • liqueurs • non-alcoholic drinks • scotch whisky • wine list
FEATURES	art • open kitchen • wine wall
NEARBY	Imperial Palace • Kabukiza
CONTACT	6-2-10 Ginza, Chuo-ku, Tokyo, 104-0061• telephone: +81.3.3575 2767 • facsimile: +81.3.3289 5937 • website: www.6eme.com

PHOTOGRAPHS COURTESY OF LE 6EME SENS D'OENON.

Mango Tree Tokyo

THIS PAGE (FROM TOP): *Dine in a sophisticated setting with a breathtaking city view; sample the best of spicy and zesty traditional Thai flavours.*

OPPOSITE: *The entrance lights up with paper lotus flowers, Thailand's national flower.*

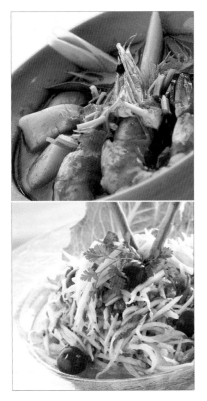

Being one of the most popular Thai restaurants in Bangkok, Mango Tree established its third outlet in the bustling city of Tokyo after opening its first overseas branch in London in 2001. Inspired by its sister restaurant that is housed in a century-old traditional Thai residence in Suriwong, central Bangkok, Mango Tree Tokyo brings the same authentic Thai cuisine to Japan in a stylish yet relaxed atmosphere. Like what the owner of Mango Tree Bangkok, Pitaya Phanphensophon, believes, 'every guest should be treated as if they were coming into your own home.'

With a splendid spot on the 35th floor of the Marunouchi Building in the heart of the metropolis, enjoying a panoramic view of the city skyline has become the norm at Mango Tree Tokyo. What makes the viewing experience different—and more spectacular—is the restaurant's floor-to-ceiling windows. Together with the soft lighting and cosy ambience, it captures perfectly the essence of Tokyo's night scene.

To enter the dining area, guests have to first walk through a narrow corridor across a see-through floor sparkling with paper lotus flowers, an experience in itself. With an interior that is synonymous with sheer style and sophistication, guests are forgiven if, for a moment, they think they have stepped into another world. Mango Tree Tokyo's simple yet contemporary décor bears a strong resemblance to that of the London outlet's equally impressive interior. Yet, with an urban setting that is part of the renowned Tokyo skyline, the restaurant retains a distinct Japanese character. In offering the internationally acclaimed home-style food from all the four major culinary regions of Thailand, Mango Tree Tokyo certainly provides a unique dining alternative for the discerning guest.

Covering the best of local flavours, the menu boasts a great variety of traditional Thai food. Popular dishes such as Som Tam Thai (Green Papaya Salad with Spicy Lime Sauce) and Thod Mun Goong (Deep Fried Breaded Shrimp Cakes served with Sweet Chilli Sauce) create a symphony of tastes that are accompanied by other appetising

dishes. For seafood lovers, sampling the Stir-fried Crab with Yellow Curry Sauce or Fried Giant River Prawn with Curry Sauce is a must. Meat connoisseurs need not fret as they get to choose from a wide range that includes pork, chicken and beef. Those with a sweet tooth will savour the enticing

desserts on offer. Traditional Thai desserts such as Fresh Mango with Sticky Rice and one of the house specials, Pavlova with Tropical Fruit and Banana Ice Cream, will leave guests wanting more.

Popular among diners, the restaurant's lunch buffet offers the same delectable Thai fare with a menu that changes every day. Its seasonal courses also refresh the palate with new menus every month. For those who want to surprise their loved ones with a birthday or anniversary bash, a special menu is available that is limited to an exclusive five parties per night.

Following the success of Mango Tree Tokyo, Mango Tree Café recently opened its doors in a popular department store in Shinjuku. Like the restaurant, the café serves authentic Thai cuisine, but this time in a more casual ambience. For the best of traditional Thai food in Tokyo, no air travel is necessary; visitors just need to take a ride up to Mango Tree Tokyo at Marunouchi.

FACTS		
	SEATS	100
	FOOD	authentic Thai
	DRINK	frozen fruit drinks • Mango Tree specials • Thai beers
	FEATURES	anniversary course menu • lunch buffet
	NEARBY	Ginza • Hibiya Park • Imperial Palace • Shimbashi • Tokyo Station
	CONTACT	35F Marunouchi Building, 2-4-1 Marunouchi, Chiyoda-ku, Tokyo, 100-6335 • telephone: +81.3.5224 5489 • facsimile: +81.3.5224 5525 • email: info@wonderland.to • website: www.mangotree.jp

My Humble House Tokyo

By day, Tokyo is a buzzing metropolis where there is no shortage of activities for visitors to engage in. After sunset, the city's numerous eating houses and watering holes spring to life, offering the perfect spots to relax and unwind.

Housed in the newly opened Zoe Ginza building, My Humble House Tokyo is located in one of the trendiest parts of a city whose landscape is constantly changing as it makes room for new and even more creative additions. Its 'new authentic' idea was created by MYU Planning & Operators Inc. in collaboration with the established Tung Lok Group of Singapore. Presenting a unique concept that combines the restaurant with a saloon and a bar, My Humble House

Tokyo is the first such restaurant in Japan to offer Singaporean cuisine. A high-end eatery that is well suited for the discerning Ginza crowd, soothing music floats gently throughout this classy and truly exceptional establishment where the air

THIS PAGE (CLOCKWISE FROM TOP): My Humble House Tokyo gives off an elegant and opulent charm; superb Singaporean cuisine in a stylish Tokyo setting make for a unique dining experience; look forward to great food accompanied by live music.

OPPOSITE (FROM LEFT): Relax and enjoy a cosy ambience enhanced by soft lighting; sample a drink or two for the perfect after dinner indulgence.

appears oblivious to the passage of time. It is no wonder then a sense of calm and timeless quality is palpable here.

The first restaurant to be opened in Japan's capital by Singapore's Tung Lok Group, My Humble House Tokyo serves Singaporean fare that offers a 'modern Chinese cuisine whose temperature has been elevated by the heat of Southeast Asia.' Using Chinese food as its base, ingredients and spices from Singapore and Malaysia are combined and prepared with a touch of French flair. The menu is created by the renowned Sam Leong, who has won several awards for his culinary skills. One of the youngest executive chefs in Singapore, Sam is Kitchen Director to all the restaurants under the Tung Lok Group and regarded as a star chef in the region.

Delectable and original dishes aside, the restaurant's stylish setting and relaxing ambience enhance its appeal, drawing a steady flow of guests every night. Incorporating black as its primary colour, the décor is neo-conservative with a modern twist. Indeed, My Humble House Tokyo exudes an elegance whose splendour sets up the perfect place for anyone seeking excellent food and entertainment for the night. In the main hall, guests can unwind and sway to the beat of tango, bossa nova, salsa and Latin jazz as live performances are held on stage. Warm and professional, the restaurant's immaculate service will round off the perfect evening.

FACTS		
	SEATS	150
	FOOD	Singaporean
	DRINK	cocktails • wine list
	FEATURES	saloon-restaurant-bar • live jazz, latin and fusion music
	NEARBY	Ginza
	CONTACT	B1 Zoe Ginza, 3-3-1 Ginza, Chuo-ku, Tokyo, 104-0061 • telephone: +81.3.5524 6166 • facsimile: +81.3.5524 6168 • e-mail: my-humble_house@my.sgn.ne.jp • website: www.mhht.jp

Sky

Even with recent developments targeted at creating more upmarket shopping hubs within Tokyo, Ginza remains the most illustrious. The internationally acclaimed Ginza-dori, the main shopping belt, houses over 10,000 stores, making it one of the city's busiest districts. With a reputation for designer trends and sophistication, well-heeled shoppers treading the streets lead the way in making Ginza a fashionable meeting spot in the centre of town.

Situated on the 16th floor of the Mitsui Garden Hotel, Sky is located right in the heart of the action. Designed by Italian Piero Lissoni, the glass-encased architecture sets an impressively contemporary tone, its spatial qualities making it part of the ukiyo-e, or the intriguingly abstract concept of the elusive 'floating world' which the hotel was built on. Remarkable views from the surrounding full-length windows are even more dramatic in the evenings when the startling array of lights illuminate the cityscape. Reflecting this urban backdrop is the restaurant's interior, a myriad of modern glass and chrome. Sharp edges and sleek lines, in both the design and furniture, give Sky a sophistication that is more than well-matched with its beautifully presented food.

Serving contemporary Italian cuisine with an emphasis on fresh, organic and seasonal vegetables, the food at Sky echoes

THIS PAGE (FROM TOP): Sky's sophisticated setting beckons; with the freshest ingredients and a tantalising menu, guests can enjoy a delicious meal safely in the knowledge that the food is good for them.
OPPOSITE: Sit back and relax on the comfortable sofas with some wine or a cocktail.

its fresh, simple yet stylish décor. Buying produce directly from organic farmers, ingredients are freshly delivered from Japan's countryside, ensuring superb quality and taste. Guests can enjoy a healthy Japanese or continental buffet breakfast that includes a wide selection of vegetables and homemade breads. Sky's lunches are just as appetising, offering a prix fixe and à la carte menu that provide a quick but welcoming respite for shoppers or businessmen who are always on the go. Dishes such as Foie Gras with Grape and Mango Sauce and deliciously handmade pastas featuring Fettuccine with Pig Cheek, Porcini and White Wine Cream are a treat for the palate. Dinner is equally memorable. With a menu that blends Japanese ingredients with Italian recipes, diners can sample great fusion fare while enjoying the superb night lights. Sky's specialities include the all-time favourite, the succulent Miyazaki Fillet Beef with Gravy Sauce. For a different

taste, diners can try Sky's special organic vegetarian course, and the chef's tasting menu, which changes seasonally.

Complete dinner by choosing a wine from more than 140 labels that have been carefully selected from Italy, France, Spain, Argentina and the US. Skilled sommeliers are also at hand to advise on the most

suitable bottle from the house red to a more in-demand vintage of a fine wine. Offering more stunning views, but of Tokyo Bay this time, the separate bar next door provides a sophisticated pre- or post-dinner cocktail. Designer sofas, contemporary furnishings and a well-stocked bar ensure a stylish end to the evening.

FACTS		
	SEATS	110
	FOOD	contemporary Italian
	DRINK	bar • lounge • cocktails • extensive wine list
	FEATURES	prix fixe lunch menu • wine sommelier
	NEARBY	Ginza
	CONTACT	16F Mitsui Garden Hotel, 8-13-1 Ginza, Chuo-ku, Tokyo, 104-0061 • telephone: +81.3.3543 3157 • facsimile: +81.3.3543 3158 • email: info@sky-ginza.com • website: www.sky-ginza.com

PHOTOGRAPHS COURTESY OF SKY.

The Oregon Bar + Grill

THIS PAGE (FROM TOP): Sample premium US beef with the spectacular Tokyo Tower in the background; the entrance's wooden décor exudes a rustic charm that is reminiscent of traditional American steakhouses.

OPPOSITE: Admire the breathtaking city skyline in an informal yet stylish setting.

Nestled among Tokyo's soaring office buildings, The Oregon Bar & Grill provides the ideal setting to satisfy any craving for Western-style steaks that locals, travellers or expatriates in Tokyo may have. An offshoot of McCormick & Schmick's chain of fine dining restaurants that are scattered all over the US, The Oregon Bar & Grill serves supreme grade beef. Named after Oregon, the state in the US which is known for its rich agriculture and booming fishing industry, the restaurant provides the juiciest and most tender US beef, freshest seafood and quality wine from a contracted winery in Oregon, all delivered directly across from the Pacific.

Situated on the dizzying 42nd-floor of the Shiodome City Center building, The Oregon Bar & Grill embraces the magnificent night view of Tokyo, capturing both the majestic Tokyo Tower and Roppongi Hills. Emulating the cosy ambience of traditional American steak houses, this restaurant in Tokyo is designed with wooden flooring and tables, but presented in chic urban fashion. The sophisticated mahogany-and-leather seats exude an opulent charm and are a perfect complement to the restaurant's classic yet stylish décor. With a spacious dining room and a bar corner, guests can indulge in the relaxing atmosphere and seek solace from the hustle and bustle of the city outside. An elite crowd, including young professionals, gathers here for a meal accompanied by superb wines and served by warm and professional English-speaking staff.

Remember to taste The Oregon Bar & Grill's signature charcoal grilled steaks of supreme grade beef. The butter-tinged steaks are cooked according to guests' preferences. Be it medium-rare or otherwise, the steak is savoured by any connoisseur meat lover. Inspired by Oregon's seafood-rich culture that is borne out of its long coastline and abundant fishing grounds, the restaurant offers some of the best seafood around. Like its counterparts in the US, the

menu at The Oregon Bar & Grill here is prepared daily to reflect the changing prices and selection at the fish market, resulting in a tantalising menu that never fails to entice guests to return for more. And as guitarists strum some old favourites from Carole King and Billy Joel in an Old West ambience, the ultimate American experience is re-created.

Like its top grade red meat, the restaurant takes as much pride in its impressive Oregon wine list. In addition to the signature Oregon organic red and white wines, the bar also serves a wide range of cocktails and alcoholic drinks such as Bourbon Jim Beam and Miller drafts. For a little variation, special menus are prepared during the festive season. During Christmas in 2006, 'Rose Christmas Nights' were held for three nights, with an excellent menu that included champagne, seafood salad, sea bream saute, veal sirloin and the like.

From formal events to casual nights out, The Oregon Bar & Grill welcomes anybody who is looking for the rich taste of American grilled cuisine, including its popular lunch buffet. Officially recognised by the Oregon state government, it is one true authentic American restaurant. And with its fine selection of Oregon wines, it offers the best of American grilled food—in an American atmosphere no less—right here in Tokyo.

FACTS		
SEATS	170	
FOOD	steak and seafood grill	
DRINK	cocktails • extensive wine list	
FEATURES	charcoal grilled steaks of supreme prime grade beef	
NEARBY	Ginza • Shimbashi	
CONTACT	42F Shiodome City Centre, 1-5-2 Higashi-Shimbashi, Minato-ku, Tokyo, 105-7142 • telephone: +81.3.6215 8585 • facsimile: +81.3.6215 8586 • email: info@wonderland.to • website: www.wonderland.to	

PHOTOGRAPHS COURTESY OF MARUHA RESTAURANT SYSTEMS CO. LTD.

Atelier Shinji

Ginza, the glamorous shopping district located in central Tokyo, is a real godsend for Tokyo's discerning dresser. The most sought-after Japanese, Italian and French brands have all chosen this prestigious spot to open their doors to the brand-conscious crowd, and it is in this niche neighbourhood that Shinji and Matico Naoi have set up their boutique, Atelier Shinji, conveniently located a stone's throw away from the famous Ginza 4-chome crossing.

Atelier Shinji's lime green flag—a dynamic contrast to its white brick entrance—beckons visitors inside. In the style of a typical Parisian atelier, the shop space is tastefully decorated with fine detailing and antique furniture. Each piece of jewellery is designed and handcrafted within the premises. The basement of this quaint shop has been converted into the couple's workshop. The two first met in Paris and later set up their own shop in Tokyo in

Each piece of jewellery is designed and handcrafted within the premises.

and floral motifs. The Ma Collection certainly does not pale in comparison. It is Matico's very own line of silver jewellery, incorporating various Japanese traditional motifs that are influenced by the four seasons. While the designs of both collections are fun and unique, they are also practical for daily use.

The ornamental leaves that hang on the walls and the rustic-looking display cases within the boutique add a cosy touch to the interior as they form a welcoming presence. Most fascinating of all is a semi-opaque display glass case in the shop that allows customers to see through, all the way down to the workshop in the basement, where the metal mould casting process takes place.

Stepping into Atelier Shinji will make for an intriguing experience. Right in the heart of bustling Tokyo, the visitor can slip away, if only for a moment, into a quiet Parisian boutique where the finest of Japanese creations can be found.

1986. Their business picked up and was particularly well received in Europe in the 1990s, though the couple have shifted their focus to the Japanese market in recent times.

The two exclusive collections found at Atelier Shinji are the proud creations of the owners. The eponymous collection by Shinji has been deeply inspired by Art Nouveau designs during his stay in Paris, evident from his elegant collection that is based on plant

FACTS

PRODUCTS	handcrafted silver and gold jewellery
FEATURES	each piece of jewellery is designed and handcrafted in the boutique
NEARBY	Ginza
CONTACT	5-13-11 Ginza, Chuo-ku, Tokyo, 104-0061 • telephone: +81.3.5565 5950 • facsimile: +81.3.5565 9771 • email: info@ateliershinji.com • website: www.ateliershinji.com

Fukumitsuya Sake Brewery

During the winter months, a sense of anticipation fills the air at the sakagura (sake cellar) of Fukumitsuya Sake Brewery. It is during this time that the kurabito, or sake brewers, start preparation for the brewing of their savoury sake, which involves mixing fresh and chilled water, together with carefully selected sake rice. At this brewery, there is a firm belief that nature forms the principal ingredient of the fermentation process of sake where natural brewing is carried out to create pure junmai (rice) sake.

The water Fukumitsuya uses is a mineral-rich water called hyakunen-sui, or one-hundred-year water. Originating from Mount Hakusan, the water has gone through a filtering process over a century before reaching the well used by the brewery. Since 1960, Fukumitsuya has exercised strict quality control with contract farmers from three different prefectures, cultivating rice of the finest quality that is used to produce their sake.

The traditional skills of homemade sake have been passed down from one generation to the next, and these precious artisanal methods are irreplaceable by modern machinery and technology. The experienced kurabito are able to immediately sense and identify any changes in the malt and yeast, and Fukumitsuya's efforts in selecting only the best ingredients produce what it believes to be sake that is 'light and full of taste.' The junmai sake leaves a pleasant aftertaste as its flavours can be fully savoured after just one sip. This, according to the brewery, is only possible by harnessing the goodness of natural brewing to its fullest.

Fukumitsuya Sake Brewery was founded in 1625 during the Edo era in Kanazawa City, an ancient castle town known for

THIS PAGE (FROM LEFT): For a taste of premium rice wine, sample Fukumitsuya's junmai sake; customers can browse through a wide range of sake products.

OPPOSITE (FROM LEFT): Stop by Ginza's bar counter for some freshly brewed sake; the store's trendy décor sets the mood for tasting delectable appetisers with sake.

In the junmai sake, the brewery has produced a sake of the finest quality.

cups and appetisers that complement the beverage. At the Tamagawa shop, the attention is shifted to products related to the process of fermentation, such as traditional food items and cosmetics. For a taste of Fukumitsuya's fine sake, shoppers can conveniently stop by the bar area in the

Kanazawa and Ginza stores. Cold as the winter months may be in Tokyo, when the kurabito prepare the junmai sake, a sip of this naturally brewed sake fills the heart with warmth. With exquisite rice wine and a unique shopping experience on offer, Fukumitsuya's sake stores are not to be missed.

traditional craftsmanship. Surrounded by the sea and mountains, it has access to superb ingredients. By returning to the roots of sake brewing with the use of natural ingredients, and by tapping the expertise of its brewers, Fukumitsuya has fine-tuned its brewing skills to perfection. In the junmai sake, the brewery has produced a sake of the finest quality.

Fukumitsuya's main shop is located in Kanazawa City, with two branches in Tokyo. The store at Ginza sells sake, sake

FACTS

PRODUCTS	sake • sake accessories • appetisers • sake cosmetics
FOOD	Japanese
DRINK	bar area
FEATURES	junmai sake • gallery
NEARBY	Ginza Station • Matsuzakaya Department Store • Mitsukoshi Department Store
CONTACT	1F, 5-5-8 Ginza, Chuo-ku, Tokyo, 104-0061 • telephone: +81.3.3569 2291 • facsimile: +81.3.3569 2291 • e-mail: ginza@fukumitsuya.co.jp • website: www.fukumitsuya.co.jp

PHOTOGRAPHS COURTESY OF FUKUMITSUYA SAKE BREWERY.

Ito-ya

Once again, Ginza is where all the happenings are in bustling Tokyo. Ginza's patrons include famous international labels that line all sides of its streets, an area in the city centre that has become synonymous with slick architecture and exclusive shopping. This celebrated list does not end with designer names; stationery can be just as fashionable—just ask Ito-ya. A perennial favourite among Tokyoites, the flagship store of this household brand makes an excellent addition to the shopping district of Ginza.

Ito-ya's origins can be traced back to 1904 when its founder, Katsutaro Ito, set up his maiden stationery store on the main street of Ginza. The small shop created history by becoming the first of its kind to put up the

English word 'stationery' on its signboard, which was considered remarkable at a time when Japanese patriotism was running high along with the imperialist mood of the day. As Ginza began to flourish, so did Ito-ya, in particular with the introduction of European

THIS PAGE (CLOCKWISE FROM TOP): **The unmistakable big red paper clip; calligraphy enthusiasts will have an indulging time browsing through a variety of brushes and ink stones; the mesmerising colours and intricate designs add to the charm of Ito-ya's interior.**

OPPOSITE: **With a brilliant range of products that includes the highly popular washi, Ito-ya has something for everyone.**

...a must-see stationery shop that can be truly fêted as a stationery wonderland.

and American stationery into the domestic market. In fact, Ito-ya's own development coincided with some of the most tumultuous times in Japan's history. The shop bounced back from the Great Kanto Earthquake of 1923 and proudly erected the resplendent seven-storey Neo-Renaissance-style Ito-ya Building in 1930. And during the chaos of World War II, Katsutaro closed the shutters of his shop that he had been running for over 40 years. After overcoming several hurdles, the Ito family finally re-opened their business in 1950, with a new building erected in 1965, the same one in which the shop is housed today. By that time, Katsutaro had retired from his position as president, having handed over the reins to his son-in-law, Yoshitaka, and grandson, Tsuneo.

In 2004, Ito-ya celebrated its centennial year in business. Instantly recognised by its company logo—the distinctive big red paper clip—an amazing array of stationery can be found at its flagship store. Ito-ya sells quality products with the most innovative and unique designs. Worth a special mention is its washi selection, which consists of over 3,000 types of Japanese paper in various materials and colours. A multitude of brushes and paper for Japanese calligraphy is also available, meeting the needs of every calligrapher, from novice to expert.

Stationery plays a part in everyone's lives, and Ito-ya's simple idea has taken root in Canada, the US and Germany, where it has established a global network. Combining international appeal with tradition, Ito-ya has reached cult status in Japan, a must-see stationery shop that can be truly fêted as a stationery wonderland.

FACTS

PRODUCTS	stationery
FEATURES	9 floors of stationery • tea lounge on the top floor • 2 annex buildings
NEARBY	Ginza
CONTACT	2 7-15 Ginza, Chuo-ku, Tokyo, 104-0061 • telephone: +81.3.3561 8311 • facsimile: +81.3.3535 7066 • email: webmaster@ito-ya.co.jp • website: www.ito-ya.co.jp

PHOTOGRAPHS COURTESY OF ITO-YA.

SCAI The Bathhouse

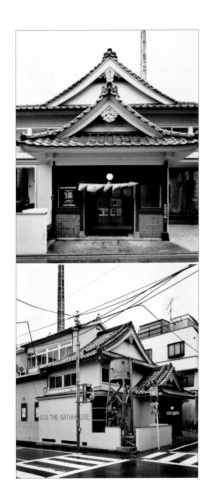

A deep sense of nostalgia fills the air at Shiraishi Contemporary Art Inc. Housed in Kashiwayu, a traditional Japanese bathhouse that was originally built in 1787, the art gallery—commonly known as SCAI The Bathhouse—opened in 1993 in the historic Yanaka district of Tokyo. Having retained much of its old-world charm, Yanaka is a popular spot among travellers, and very much an attraction in itself. Temples that date as far back as the 17th century are just some of the quaint places that can be found in this cultural hub of the city. Similarly, visitors will be intrigued by the traditional candies and rice crackers that are sold on the old shopping street of Yanaka Ginza.

The same rustic beauty can be found in SCAI's Kashiwayu, whose original structure has been carefully preserved and rightly so. Its beautiful exterior, with the curved Japanese tiled roofing, antique wall tiles and wooden columns, stands out as a work of art on its own. The chimney pipe, water tank and shoe locker that were once used in the bathhouse will certainly fascinate guests. Inside, the big skylight on the 7-m- (23-ft-) high ceiling sends light flooding in, creating a brightly-lit art gallery that is perfect for showcasing exhibits.

Spanning the entire period of the development of contemporary art from the 1950s to the present, SCAI represents a diverse group of artists. Responsible for building up the arts scene after World War II and pioneering Japanese contemporary art, Genpei Akasegawa dominated the 1960s with his bold and controversial works. In the late 1980s, Japanese art came into prominence and artists such as Toshikatsu Endo and Mariko Mori led the way in international acclaim. Now represented by SCAI, they continue to globetrot, holding their exhibitions in galleries and art fairs around the world. Renowned Japanese artists, including Nobuko Tsuchiya and Tatsuo Miyajima, also share a strong rapport with SCAI, with whom they frequently exhibit their works.

Alongside this prestigious list of artists, SCAI seeks out new young talent to groom and is currently working with the increasingly

prominent Kohei Nawa. Nawa's recent exhibition displayed objects bought from Internet auction sites, which he either covered with transparent beads or placed into prism boxes to transform the objects back into their original digital image, with an artistic touch and a different medium this time.

Keeping a finger on the global arts' pulse, SCAI's interests extend beyond the domestic scene and they have hosted international artists such as Anish Kapoor, Martin Puryear, Dzine, Jenny Holzer, Lee Bul, Julian Opie, David Tremlett, Jeppe Hein and Lee Ufan. With monthly exhibitions showcasing this diverse wealth of talent, from the natural landscapes and silhouettes of Toru Kamiya's oil and acrylic paintings to the extreme and sometimes violent LED signs from American artist Jenny Holzer, SCAI clearly embodies the dynamism and avant-garde spirit of contemporary art.

THIS PAGE (FROM LEFT): 'Love Junkee', 2006, an artwork by Dzine; 'PixCell-Bambi', 2005, Kohei Nawa's representation of an 'Internet bambi'.

OPPOSITE (FROM LEFT): SCAI's quaint gallery exudes rustic charm; the 'Films and Painting' exhibition, by Julian Opie.

FACTS		
	PRODUCTS	local and international contemporary art
	FEATURES	traditional 200-year-old building • viewing room in Roppongi • monthly exhibitions
	NEARBY	National Museum of Western Art • Nezu Station • Tokyo National Museum
	CONTACT	6-1-23 Yanaka, Taito-ku, Tokyo, 110-0001 • telephone: +81.3.3821 1144 • facsimile: +81.3.3821 3553 • email: info@scaithebathhouse.com • website: www.scaithebathhouse.com

PHOTOGRAPHS COURTESY OF SHIRAISHI CONTEMPORARY ART INC.

Tasaki Shinju

Japan is a country of many facets. Its beautiful cherry blossoms, unique cuisine, serene temples and hot springs have attracted visitors worldwide. Similarly, the sea forms an integral part of this island country. What has emerged from these surrounding waters has propelled Japan to international stardom on several fronts. One of these precious products is the pearl.

Tasaki Shinju is a world leader in these beautiful gems of nature. Founded more than 50 years ago, Tasaki is an integrated pearl enterprise that covers the overall operation of pearl manufacturing, from pearl culturing and processing to sales. With such a setup, it is capable of projecting the beauty of pearls internationally. 'Without dreams, nothing can be realised' is the company motto, driving its ambitions of becoming a global jeweller by opening up new frontiers of jewellery. With extensive experience in the pearl industry, Tasaki has expanded its business into one that includes diamonds and various precious stones and metals.

Not only does Tasaki produce pearls of superb quality through its elaborate techniques of pearl cultivation that span a number of years, it is the only company in Japan which is a sightholder in The Diamond Trading Company, the world's largest supplier of rough diamonds. All of Tasaki's jewellery showcases original designs created by in-house designers who have won various awards in national and international jewellery design competitions, being an unprecedented 20-time winner at

THIS PAGE: Expertly crafted and beautifully designed pieces.

OPPOSITE (FROM LEFT): Tasaki offers style, sophistication and quality; visitors will be spoilt for choice by the glittering array of jewellery at the flagship store.

the prestigious DTC Diamond International design contest. With top-notch designers and skilled craftsmen, it is unsurprising that the company's quality products have enticed many jewellery enthusiasts.

Tasaki owns retail outlets throughout the major cities of Japan. Excellent service is a norm in these shops as well-trained staff provide invaluable advice to customers. Clients are given the flexibility to make purchases through other means like trade fairs and export services. In October 1997, Tasaki opened Tasaki Jewellery Tower in the celebrated shopping district of Ginza where famous local and international brands line the streets. Tasaki's flagship store occupies the world's largest floor space, as products ranging from high-end jewellery to intricate gifts adorn its stunning showroom. With glittering pearls, coloured stones and over 25,000 pieces—including an exceptional range of bridal jewellery—lining the showcases, it is every jewellery aficionado's paradise. A gorgeous pearl and crystal chandelier worth 300 million yen lights up the main entrance, while on the fifth floor, guests will find a jewellery museum with interesting exhibits that tell the intriguing history of gems. A jewel of a city with its many attractions, a visit to Tokyo will not be complete without stopping by Tasaki Shinju.

FACTS

PRODUCTS	bridal jewellery • coloured stone • diamond • pearl • South Sea pearl
FEATURES	global jewellery company • wide range of products and sales network • overseas stores in China, Hong Kong and Taiwan
NEARBY	Ginza
CONTACT	5-7-5 Ginza, Chuo-ku, Tokyo, 104-8010 • telephone: +81.3.5561 8879 • facsimile: +81.3.5561 0748 • website: www.tasaki.co.jp

PHOTOGRAPHS COURTESY OF TASAKI SHINJU.

The Spa at Mandarin Oriental, Tokyo

Covering the top two floors of the hotel, The Spa at Mandarin Oriental, Tokyo welcomes hotel guests as well as local residents. With sister spas in Bangkok, New York and London, The Spa has been rated by *Condé Nast Traveller* to be among the top 10 urban day spas in the world.

Treatment suites at The Spa are sleek and modern. A glass wall offers a sharp and dramatic view of the cityscape while the other walls are covered in soft fabrics decorated with soothing motifs of nature. Each suite contains a different feature, ranging from a rasul room to a shower and a deep marble bath where guests can relax while taking in the sights of Tokyo from the 37th floor.

To avoid disappointment, reservations are recommended. Guests are encouraged to arrive an hour before their session to allow sufficient time to maximise The Spa's excellent facilities that include dry saunas, steam rooms and water lounges.

THIS PAGE (CLOCKWISE FROM TOP): *Experienced and friendly staff at the reception make guests feel immediately welcome; sauna with a view; the Serenity Suite offers an intimate setting with the magnificent Mount Fuji in the background.*
OPPOSITE: *Relax and take in the spectacular skyline in the spacious Harmony Suite.*

The Spa's exotic treatments are derived from philosophies from around the world, including Europe, China, Thailand, India and Arabia. There are more than 40 luxurious massages, body scrubs and facials tailored to address each guest's personal needs. The Spa's signature treatment, Oriental Harmony, begins with a soothing footbath in purifying waters that relaxes both mind and body. Next, two therapists work on a body scrub and massage before the treatment ends with a simultaneous head and foot massage, leaving guests feeling fully re-energised. Holistic facials are suitably named Awaken, Calm, Illuminate, Hydrate and Stimulate as they provide a lavishly moisturising and refreshing experience. Specialised herbal therapies include the deeply cleansing and invigorating Azuki Ritual, where the natural components of azuki beans are combined with sea salt, sesame seeds, patchouli, vetiver, ginger and geranium for a

softening and conditioning body scrub. This is followed by a relaxing oil treatment to moisturise and nourish the body.

At the dry sauna, there is space to relax and enjoy the astounding view of the city before cooling off by the ice fountain that

helps to tone and stimulate the immune system. Indulgence extends beyond the nine treatment rooms with vitality pools, water lounges and crystal steam rooms. For anyone seeking the ultimate relaxation, the rejuvenating experience of The Spa beckons.

FACTS

PRODUCTS	signature treatments • body therapy • body treatments • facials • manicures • pedicures
FEATURES	water lounges • crystal steam rooms • gym • ice fountain • dry sauna
NEARBY	Ginza • Imperial Palace • Nihonbashi Bridge • Tokyo Central Station
CONTACT	Mandarin Oriental, Tokyo, 2-1-1 Nihonbashi-Muromachi, Chuo-ku, Tokyo, 103-8328 • telephone: +81.3.3270 8300 • facsimile: +81.3.3270 8308 • email: motyo-spaconcierge@mohg.com • website: www.mandarinoriental.com/tokyo

PHOTOGRAPHS COURTESY OF MANDARIN ORIENTAL, TOKYO.

Mejiro

Mejiro-dori

Takadanobaba

Shin-Mejiro-dori

● ─── > Four Seasons Hotel Tokyo
        at Chinzan-so

Ueno

tokyointhehills

LaQua ●

Tokyo Dome

Shinokubo

Akihabara

Yasukuni Shrine

Yasukuni-dori

The National Museum
of Modern Art, Tokyo

Shinjuku

Takebashi

Crafts Gallery,
The National Museum
of Modern Art, Tokyo

Yoyogi

> **Kurayamizaka Miyashita
  Restaurants**
> **The Ritz Carlton**
> **Super Dining Zipangu**

Tokyo
Station

Meiji-dori

Imperial Palace /
Nijubashi

Meiji Shrine

Akasaka-
Mitsuke

Sotobori-dori

Yoyogi
Park

Harajuku

Aoyama-dori

Sumidagawa River

Pleats Please Issey
Miyake Aoyama
Omotesando Hills
Fuji-Torii
Issey Miyake Aoyama

Gaien-Higashi-dori

Roppongi-dori

Shinbashi

Nogizaka
Station

Omotesando

Omotesando Avenue

National
Art Center

Roppongi

> Citabria
> Roti
> Furutoshi

Dresscamp
Stair

Gaien-Nishi-dori

Shibuya

Tokyo Tower

Roppongi Hills
> Grand Hyatt Tokyo

Azabu-Juban

Hamamatsucho

> Pacific Currents
> Badou-R
> Den Aquaroom Aoyama
> Mizuma Art Gallery
> The Westin Tokyo

Meiji-dori

Ebisu

Metropolitan Expressway

Tamachi

Nakameguro

Yamate-dori

Ebisu Garden Palace ●

Komazawa-dori

*Tokyo
Bay*

Metropolitan Expressway

Tokyo Metropolitan
Teien Art Museum

Meguro

N

Shinagawa

Legend	
	Expressway
	Main roads
	JR Line
	Private Line
	Subway
	Monorail
	Stations
	Water

0 km   0.5   1   1.5   2 km

the emperor's backyard

Japan's emperor stands at the centre of time and space. This is not a declaration of emperor worship. It is a simple statement of fact, and one easily checked on a calendar or map.

Each year on the official Japanese calendar is labelled according to its place in the relevant imperial reign. Emperor Akihito, the current monarch, was enthroned in 1989, which is also called Heisei 1. The year 1990 was Heisei 2, the year 1991 Heisei 3, and so on. Emperors change their names when they die, and Heisei is how Akihito will officially be known in generations to come. (The previous emperor, remembered as Hirohito by the rest of the world, is officially called Showa in Japan.) But the Western style of numbering years is also widely used, so people will understand 2007 as readily as Heisei 19.

On any map of central Tokyo, you will find a large green area, more than 1 km (⅔ mile) wide, right in the middle. These are the grounds of the Imperial Palace, where Emperor Akihito officially resides. Surrounded by broad moats, the Palace faces east, towards the older part of Tokyo, which is built on the water. But its grounds rise sharply on their western side, making them part of the relatively younger western half of the city, which is built in the hills. This means the banks of the western moat are extremely high, although the eastern banks are almost low enough for passers-by to reach down and touch the water. There are large areas where visitors are free to wander in the Palace's outer gardens, but most of the extensive grounds are off limits to the public.

The common people are briefly allowed a bit further into the Palace grounds during the New Year holidays, when the Emperor and his family greet them from a balcony in one of the few scheduled public Imperial appearances of the year. The crowds flock back to the Palace again for another greeting on the Emperor's birthday, which is also a national holiday. The current Emperor happens to have been born on December 23, meaning that his meetings with the masses begin and end each of the years that share his future name.

PAGE 92: A businessman walks through a tunnel near the Roppongi Hills complex, one of the major new commercial and cultural centres of Tokyo.

THIS PAGE: In the centre of Tokyo's energy and bustle, a garden near the Imperial Palace is a discrete island of calm.

OPPOSITE: Swans glide past Nijubashi Bridge, an entryway to the Imperial Palace.

Under Japan's present-day Constitution, the Emperor plays a purely symbolic role, but that green part of the map on which he lives marks the centre of Chiyoda Ward as well as the centre of Tokyo itself. And Chiyoda Ward is a part of the city that is full of people and institutions whose power is much more than just symbolic.

chiyoda ward: centres of power

Chiyoda Ward, wrapped around the Imperial Palace like a giant concrete moat made of buildings and streets, is one of the smallest of the 23 wards that comprise central Tokyo, but it is also one of the most densely packed with important places. Immediately to the east of the Palace, this ward contains Tokyo Station and the media and retail centres of Marunouchi. To the south of the Palace is the bureaucratic enclave of Kasumigaseki, where the major government ministries have their headquarters. The Japan Patent Office and the Metropolitan Police Department are based here, and the US Embassy stands nearby, just outside the Chiyoda Ward boundary.

Southwest of the Palace is Nagatacho, dominated by the ziggurat-roofed National Diet Building, where Japan's elected lawmakers debate everything from fiscal policy to sending troops overseas. The Shusho Kantei (the Prime Minister's official residence) and the Cabinet Office are also here. Many a power lunch has been consumed at the top-flight restaurants that serve the elite of Nagatacho, such as Super Dining Zipangu.

The parts of Chiyoda Ward west of the Palace are home to the Japanese Supreme Court and the embassies of Britain, Ireland, Israel, South Africa and the Vatican. This area is also where you will find the Hotel New Otani, and luxuries such as the patisserie by Pierre Hermé. This French chef is noted for perfecting macaroons in a plethora of flavours and, complete with a Japanese touch, this includes green tea.

North of the Palace is a Chiyoda Ward institution that demonstrates how even symbols can sometimes hold a genuine power. This is Yasukuni Shrine, a Shinto military memorial built in the late 19th century to revere the souls of those who gave their lives for the sake of the nation. During and after World War II, the official roll of the honoured dead received some controversial additions, including convicted war criminals. A museum on the shrine grounds retells the history of the war from a distinctly nationalistic point of view. Japanese politicians, including prime ministers, have provoked diplomatic incidents by paying their respects at the shrine despite protests from Japan's neighbours, especially China and South Korea.

Further north, just a few steps beyond Chiyoda Ward's boundaries, is a power centre of a much happier kind—the Tokyo Dome baseball stadium. With the game a national obsession, the Dome is home to the Yomiuri Giants, one of five professional teams based in the greater Tokyo area. The Giants' winning record over the past several decades, especially in the annual Japan Series championship, dwarfs all the rest. The building itself is an engineering marvel. The vast roof, resembling a giant quilt, is supported entirely by air pressure provided by constantly turning fans. The 55,000-seat venue is also a musical power site, which in the 2000s alone has hosted concerts by such international titans as Madonna, Paul McCartney, Bon Jovi, Aerosmith and the Rolling Stones. Moody heart-throb Ken Hirai filled the place with screaming fans, and domestic pop giants such as SMAP, Kinki Kids and B'z have each played the dome numerous times.

The nation's ongoing shopping mall regeneration touched upon Tokyo Dome in 2003 with the opening of its multi-storey mall, LaQua. Home to about 70 shops and restaurants, the mall features a

THIS PAGE (FROM TOP): Yasukuni Shrine is a place of homage to Japan's casualties of war and a focus of political controversy; home to the Yomiuri Giants baseball team, Tokyo Dome is a giant in its own right.
OPPOSITE: The National Diet Building's distinctive roof, not to mention its political importance, ensures that it always stands out.

spa on its upper floors, which receives a constant supply of hot spring water that is piped from underground. Outside the mall, excitement hangs in the air with the mammoth roller coaster that jumps over the mall's roof and through LaQua's 'Big O'. While numerous monumental Ferris wheels have been built in Japan in recent years, this one must take the prize for most original. A gigantic revolving hoop devoid of hub or spokes, it's an engineering marvel on a par with the Dome itself.

quiet retreats

In an abrupt change of atmosphere, the buzz of shoppers and the shrieks of roller coaster riders on the east side of Tokyo Dome give way to the peace and quiet of a tranquil Japanese garden on its west side. This is Koishikawa Korakuen, which dates back to the 1600s. Large enough to contain several ponds and forested pathways, the garden is rarely visited by the crowds from the other side.

This leafy oasis is an apt introduction to the areas further north and west, which are mostly quiet residential neighbourhoods, within easy reach of the more energetic parts of town, yet private enough to provide a welcome retreat from them. These zones of serenity do hold some surprises, though, and one of them is St. Mary's Cathedral.

Built in 1963 to replace the original wooden structure that was destroyed during World War II, this is the main Catholic church in a city better known for temples and shrines. The building starts with a traditional cross-shaped floor plan, but above ground level things immediately become quite different. The outer walls swoop upward and inward to meet in very narrow roofs, and the outward end of each roof is higher than the portions at the centre of the cross. Architect Kenzo Tange, who died in 2005, once said that he wanted to use modern technology to recreate the "heaven-aspiring

THIS PAGE: A red footbridge stands out from the foliage in the Koishikawa Korakuen Garden.

OPPOSITE (FROM TOP): The crooked path of a rustic walkway at Koishikawa Korakuen ensures that visitors will slow down to appreciate the scenery; Kenzo Tange's 'heaven-aspiring' St. Mary's Cathedral has been likened to a white dove.

grandeur and ineffably mystical spaces" he had found in the medieval cathedrals of Europe. While those churches had solid roofs and stained-glass windows in the walls, his has solid walls and skylights in the roof. The resulting play of light across the austere interior does lend a certain mystical atmosphere.

Heaven-aspiring grandeur takes many forms, some of which can be found across the street from St. Mary's, at the chic Four Seasons Hotel Tokyo at Chinzan-so. Amenities here include a spa with a crescent-shaped pool where you may float on your back and gaze heaven-ward through a crystalline skylight. The hotel grounds include one of the most famous gardens in Tokyo, where white waterfalls and green moss are accented by pink cherry blossoms in the spring and red Japanese maple leaves in the autumn.

Continuing northwest through this quiet and almost exclusively low-rise part of the city, you may eventually hear the 'ding-ding' of a passing tram on the Toden Arakawa Line, a charming throwback to an earlier time. But beyond the tracks, the Sunshine 60 building, so named for its number of floors, rises towards the clouds as if to signal your sudden arrival in a very different part of town.

ikebukuro and shinjuku: high-rise tokyo

Tokyoites tend to describe places in reference to the nearest railway line, and the Yamanote Line, which loops around central Tokyo in a great oval, is referred to a lot. This train line forms the backbone of a high-rise corridor of important places on the western side of the city, including Shinjuku, Harajuku and Shibuya.

Sunshine City, near Ikebukuro Station on the Yamanote Line, marks the northern end of this corridor. Sunshine City is an office, hotel and shopping complex that also includes an aquarium, affording visitors the bizarre experience of watching trained seals perform on a 10th-floor

THIS PAGE (FROM LEFT): *Love is a big deal in Nishi Shinjuku, an area full of offices and luxury hotels; the grand Tokyo Metropolitan Government Building, also in Nishi Shinjuku, is even bigger. Here it is lit in Olympic colours, reflecting an official ambition to be the host city in 2016.*
OPPOSITE (FROM TOP): *A mural showing Doromi-chan, the cartoon mascot for Shinjuku's MyLord shopping complex; the shiny roof of a taxi reflects Shinjuku's nocturnal energy.*

urban rooftop. The tallest building in the complex, Sunshine 60, offers spectacular views of the city, especially of the forest of skyscrapers in Shinjuku, not far to the south.

Two of the world's largest department stores stand on opposite sides of Ikebukuro Station, as if constantly challenging each other. This impression is more than a flight of fancy; the two stores—flagships of the Seibu and Tobu chains—were founded decades ago by a pair of wealthy half-brothers-turned-business-rivals. Each ran a railroad with an Ikebukuro terminus—it's a very big and busy station—and each of them wanted to give his passengers a special reason to come here. To this day, shoppers still arrive by the trainload every hour, eager to discover which store has the best deals on designer luxury items on its upper floors, and which one offers the more tempting gourmet treats in it vast, multi-countered basement food halls.

From here, the Yamanote Line trains head south to Shinjuku, a political nerve centre, major business district and mecca for shoppers. The Isetan department store has its flagship store a few blocks east of the station, an operation so big that it occupies three adjacent buildings. And the Marui department store has five outlets scattered across the same general area, each with a different speciality. Marui's 'In The Room' store is a must for anyone who wants to keep abreast of chic Japanese interior design. Mitsukoshi has a major branch here, too. A pedestrian bridge high up in the sky connects the Takashimaya department store's 14-storey Shinjuku branch to a six-storey Kinokuniya bookstore across the street. On the west side of Shinjuku Station stand the Odakyu and Keio department stores, which work hand in hand with eponymous rail lines that have their termini here.

All of this shopping activity, especially when neon-lit at night, makes for a very gratifying view from the observation deck of the 48-storey Tokyo Metropolitan Government Building, which stands a few blocks further west. After all, when business is booming, so is the tax base and a lot of tax money went into the 1988–91 construction of this building. The investment has arguably proven worth it, as this distinctive Kenzo Tange-designed tower—which actually

splits into two mirror-image towers at the 33rd floor—has come to stand as an icon of Tokyo itself. The excellent animated film *Tokyo Godfathers*, a critical but ultimately affectionate examination of contemporary Japanese society, uses the building's looming shape and twinkling lights as a backdrop for the opening scene.

This building joined a small cluster of Shinjuku skyscrapers when it opened, but the area has since grown more crowded, with new high-rise hotels and corporate offices going up all the time. Especially noteworthy—and another by Kenzo Tange—is the Shinjuku Park Tower, built to resemble a row of three nearly identical towers pressed together side by side. With each one taller than the next, their roofs resemble a literal stairway to heaven. A shopping arcade is located on the first floors and higher up, The Park Hyatt Tokyo, the setting for the movie *Lost in Translation*, occupies the top 14 floors of this 52-storey masterpiece.

Another new Shinjuku landmark is the NTT DoCoMo Yoyogi Building, which resembles a miniature version of the Empire State Building—if 28 floors can be considered miniature. The building was completed in 2000, and a gigantic clock was later installed near the top of it, reportedly making it the biggest clock tower on earth.

As southbound Yamanote Line trains pass beneath this towering timepiece on their way out of Shinjuku, they're just minutes away from Harajuku Station, entryway to a neighbourhood with chicness to spare.

omotesando: fashion avenue

Tree-lined Omotesando, which runs east from Harajuku Station to the Minami-Aoyama neighbourhood, has long been described as the Champs-Élysées of Tokyo. For many years, this elegant nickname was arguably more aspirational than descriptive, but

THIS PAGE: An abundance of colourful signs appears to threaten Shinjuku pedestrians and train passengers with information overload.

OPPOSITE: As three young men pause on the sidewalk, Shinjuku's Friday night bustle flows around them.

nowadays Omotesando is undeniably a world-class destination for well-groomed shoppers. Just over 1 km (⅔ mile) long, the spacious boulevard is crammed with popular and high-end stores for brands such as Burberry, Fendi and Ralph Lauren. Legendary Japanese designer Hanae Mori, who has her mirror-walled headquarters on this street, remains a leading force in fashion with such innovations as a robot mannequin that raises its arms to show off her trademark butterfly designs. Fellow fashion giant Issey Miyake has several stores in the area, each focusing on his different lines of clothing, and Rei Kawakubo's Comme des Garçons also has a showroom here. But it's not all about clothes. You can buy jewellery from Cartier, or quality Japanese antiques at Fuji-Torii. Younger, up-and-coming Japanese designers also understand that this is the place to be, and street fashion as well as haute couture has a presence in the area. Mihara Yasuhiro, who designs for Puma as well as clothing under his own Sosu brand, has two shops here.

Street label A Bathing Ape (or Bape, for short) has a store just off the main avenue at its Minami-Aoyama end, where shoes parade around on a rotary sushi-style conveyor belt. It won an extra degree of cool—as if it needed it—when Eric Clapton gave Bape creator Nigo a nationally televised endorsement during a 2006 tour of Japan. Clapton, a friend of the single-name designer, also gave a shout-out to Nigo's mentor, the streetwear godfather Hiroshi Fujiwara.

Taishi Nobukuni, a graduate of London's St Martin's College, is a Japanese designer who's equally adept at designing clothes for the office (as creative director of the Takeo Kikuchi menswear brand) or the street (at his own funky shop called 13, also in Minami-Aoyama). He also knows how to create a stir, such as when he dressed his models in black for a 2006 show and sent them onto the catwalk in the dark, lit only by

blinking lights. At another of his shows the same year, models in fake fur appeared walking dogs in real fur (their own). Elsewhere along Omotesando, every phase of the fashion spectrum is covered, from the sturdy-looking denim casual wear at 45rpm to the unapologetic glamour of Toshikazu Iwaya's Dresscamp.

As in Ginza, the buildings along Omotesando are every bit as chic as their contents. The Swiss firm Herzog and de Meuron, responsible for London's Tate Modern, designed the Prada store to resemble a transparent quartz crystal wrapped in a diamond-patterned fishnet, breaking up the view of the interior in an irregular way that tempts shoppers to come inside for a closer look. Japanese architect Jun Aoki, who has designed several Louis Vuitton stores, arranged their Omotesando outlet to resemble randomly stacked luggage—right down to draping its components in a chain-mail skin that looks like highly magnified fabric.

A major addition to the avenue's landscape, the Omotesando Hills shopping mall, opened in 2006. Designed by celebrity architect Tadao Ando, it is another of the Mori family. Occupying a wedge-shaped piece of land, this multi-storey structure makes the most of its relatively narrow space by arranging shops along a spiralling walkway around a long, triangular atrium. Various eateries occupy the upper levels, while a futuristic automated wine bar rests below the ground. In between is a range of cosmetics and clothing shops, including one that specialises in designer wear for dogs—either off the rack or made to order.

The glittery façades on Omotesando are just part of the story. The street serves as the backbone to a commercial neighbourhood of considerable depth. To explore the narrow, often charmingly crooked back streets that branch off the avenue on either side is to discover an endless array of funky little shops, independent boutiques, chic hair salons, and enticing restaurants and cafes.

THIS PAGE: *All eyes are on the catwalk as models parade the latest Dresscamp fashions.*

OPPOSITE (FROM LEFT): *The Prada store on Omotesando resembles a giant, multifaceted crystal; t-shirts pass by in a moving display of a store window.*

The Montoak Café, which owes its tremendously cool and industrial look to young architect and interior designer Ishiro Katami, is a good spot to take a breather. And at the end of the day, chic watering holes in the area include Stair and Den Aquaroom. Dinner choices include Nobu Tokyo, a restaurant in Minami Aoyama created by super chef and Hollywood actor Nobu Matsuhisa. (Didn't you know? He had small parts in *Casino*, *Memoirs of a Geisha* and *Austin Powers in Goldmember*.)

a flamboyant subculture

Most Omotesando area fashion establishments cater to adults (often those at the young and trendy end of the spectrum), but one street not far away is constantly teeming with teens. This is Takeshita-dori, a thronging lane that parallels the first several blocks of Omotesando to the north near Harajuku Station, a place where Tokyo's hippest high-schoolers and university students come to update their wardrobes while their elders do the same thing a few blocks south.

The most eye-catching form of weekend wear for young people, especially girls, is in a category called cos-play, a Japanese abbreviation of the English words costume and play. Cos-play enthusiasts dress up in elaborate outfits, very often homemade, that turn them into figures of fantasy, usually drawn from the world of manga and anime but sometimes completely original. A gothic version of Little Bo Peep, which calls for layers of flouncy black lace, seems to be a perennial theme, but don't be surprised if you also see vampires, robots, cat women, fetishised variations of starched white nurses' uniforms, or even schoolgirls brandishing exotic weapons in the manner of Chiaki Kuriyama's mace-swinging character from the film *Kill Bill, Vol. 1*. Male cos-players are less common, but they sometimes can be seen as spiky-haired anime heroes, androgynous rock stars, or moustached Mario, the Nintendo video game mascot.

Cos-players don't mind public attention, but aside from their unusual mode of dress many of them do little to actively draw a crowd, instead merely enjoying the company of their fellow enthusiasts. That hasn't stopped entrepreneurs from cashing in on the

phenomenon by opening cos-play cafés, usually with a French maid theme, where costumed waitresses serve their customers. Authentic cos-players turn out in droves to celebrate special events such as manga conventions and video game trade shows, but on ordinary weekends cos-players congregate in a few favourite spots. They are likeliest to be found on and beyond the bridge leading across the train tracks from Harajuku Station toward Yoyogi Park and the National Yoyogi Stadium.

The mollusc-roofed stadium is yet another Kenzo Tange creation, and was built for the 1964 Tokyo Summer Olympics, which served, in the eyes of many, as Japan's welcome back into the family of nations after the end of World War II. Japan nowadays has little that it needs to prove in terms of international prestige, but the Tokyo Metropolitan Government has been campaigning to host its second Olympics for several years now. Stay tuned.

Aside from people watching, the main attraction of Yoyogi Park is the Meiji Shrine, which is surrounded by 70 hectares (173 acres) of wooded area. Dedicated to Emperor Meiji, the shrine is reached via a long gravel walkway that passes beneath a towering torii (temple gate) marked only by the simple chrysanthemum crest of the Imperial family. As one strolls along the path through the woods towards the shrine, the hustle and bustle of the nearby shopping area—and the surreality of the nearby cos-play scene—quietly fades away.

scintillating shibuya

But for those who thrive on hustle and bustle, the most energetic of Tokyo's neighbourhoods, Shibuya, is just one quick Yamanote Line stop away. Stepping out of Shibuya Station in the evening, one is confronted with a mountainous landscape of electric lights that gives Las Vegas a run for its money. Brilliantly lit buildings form a canyon-like wall around Shibuya Crossing, a five-lane-wide intersection that is swarmed by thousands of pedestrians with every cycle of its traffic lights. Corporate logos and ad slogans glow and flash wherever you look. Three of the buildings

THIS PAGE: *A Harajuku girl wearing two fringe fashion themes—a gothic colour scheme and platform shoes.*
OPPOSITE (FROM TOP): *A street band is part of the Shinjuku scene; Yoyogi Park, a popular hangout for the young and eccentric.*

...the hustle and bustle of the nearby shopping area... quietly fades away.

have video screens several metres high built into their façades, each playing its own continuous loop of music videos and commercial messages. The illuminated glass lifts rising and descending on the side of the 40-storey Cerulean Tower, a hotel and office building, add yet another note of brightness and motion to the scene.

Surprisingly, the most popular part of this epic, kinetic scene is something small and quiet. That is a statue of Hachiko, Japan's most famous dog. Hachiko, a stocky, curly-tailed Akita with one flopped-over ear, waited for his master outside the gate of Shibuya Station every evening until one day in 1925 when the man never came home, having died of a sudden stroke during the day. But Hachiko continued to visit the station each evening until his own death in 1935, becoming a legend in his own lifetime for his unshakeable loyalty. His story has been retold on film and even in school textbooks, but the best-known image of Hachiko is the life-sized statue of him that stands near the station entrance, one of the most popular meeting spots in Tokyo.

The Shibuya neighbourhood caters to the desires of teenage girls and young women, making it a good place to watch as fashion trends come and go in that mercurial demographic. Shibuya is a fashion fusion reactor, and its glowing core can be found behind the eight-storey cylindrical façade of the 109 building. It resembles a department store at first glance, but instead of being a single large business, 109 is actually dozens of tiny retailers gathered to form a conglomerate organism not unlike a coral reef. Depending on shoppers' whims, some parts of the reef may flourish while others fade.

In the 1990s, the customers were likely to be wearing short skirts to show off their loose socks—leg-warmer-style apparel so baggy that they need to be held in place with special sock glue to keep them from pooling around the wearer's ankles. Around the turn of the century, Shibuya became the chief haunt of fashionable young women sashaying the shops atop spike-heeled boots and vertiginous platform shoes. Further into the 2000s, the neighbourhood has become the natural habitat for aficionados of the kogyaru look—girls and young women wearing pale or even white lipstick, eyeliner and nail polish, creating a sharp contrast with their tanning-booth-darkened skin. Often dyeing

THIS PAGE (FROM TOP): The entryway to one of Shibuya's countless little clothing stores; people feel so attached to the famous dog Hachiko that they sometimes decorate his statue.

OPPOSITE: A procession of white-robed Shinto priests passes beneath the monumental torii gate of the Meiji Shrine.

their hair brown, blonde or even grey, kogyaru look almost like photographic negatives of ordinary Japanese women. There's no telling what wild new look will come next. Perhaps something will burst out of the cos-play underground and into the mainstream. But whatever the next big boom may be, Shibuya is where the fuse will be lit.

tokyo after dark

It's a shame to be all dressed up with nowhere to go, but in Shibuya that's rarely a problem. The area is a major locus of the Tokyo club scene. The scene is a bipolar affair, with techno fans on one side gravitating toward the sounds typified by uber-DJ Ken Ishii, and nu-jazz fans on the other following the DJ brothers Shuya and Yoshihiro Okino, better known as Kyoto Jazz Massive.

Ishii plays frequently in Shibuya at Womb, a club known for its line-up of cutting-edge artists, especially in the drum 'n' bass genre. Kyoto Jazz Massive, meanwhile, appear regularly at The Room, also in Shibuya. Another popular dance haven is the stunningly cool La Fabrique, which combines good music with good food. (They make a divine crème brûlée.) In the nearby Daikanyama neighbourhood, Air—the club seen in *Lost in Translation*—has a reputation as a good place to see up-and-coming club acts, as the management is said to have a real eye for talent. Detroit techno pioneer Jeff Mills, who has also played at Womb, helped introduce another Shinjuku club, the Liquid Room, to the world when he cut a live album there in the 1990s. The club is still famous, but has since split, with one half moving to Ebisu under the old name and the other opening in Daikanyama as Unit.

The Roppongi neighbourhood is another western-Tokyo clubbing hotspot. An evening here might begin at the Heartland bar, a popular spot for high-flying Japanese and expats to drink and network in the Roppongi Hills complex, before moving on to Super Deluxe, a funky, stripped down, bare concrete basement venue full of far-out people and an edgy live improv music scene. Yellow, the oldest of Tokyo's major dance clubs, is also nearby.

lucky ebisu

There's lucky, and then there is lucky, and Ebisu is one lucky god. According to Japanese mythology, there are seven gods of good luck, but the average person would be very hard pressed to name more than a couple of them. One name no one ever forgets, however, is that of the lucky god Ebisu—Patron of Seafarers and symbol of prosperity for business. It could be his chubby, smiling face that makes him so popular, or it could be the fact that he is usually depicted as a fisherman who has just caught a plump, tasty-looking bream. But the real key to his popularity is probably that he was lucky enough to get a brand of beer named after him, along with the Tokyo neighbourhood where it was first brewed back in 1887.

THIS PAGE (FROM TOP): *Cool young things dance the night away at Yellow in Roppongi; the jolly god Ebisu has a Tokyo neighbourhood and a major brand of beer named after him.*

OPPOSITE: *Shibuya has several large buildings whose façades double as video screens, including this one that displays a walking dinosaur.*

Ebisu is the Yamanote Line's next stop south from Shibuya, and the first thing passengers arriving at this station will see is that its lighting fixtures feature rows of lanterns shaped like beer kegs that are adorned with pictures of the local patron deity. A long series of moving sidewalks leads still further south to Yebisu Garden Place, a spacious shopping, commercial and entertainment complex that includes the corporate headquarters of Sapporo Breweries. The public areas, arranged around a wide, sunken plaza, include boutiques, a beer-themed restaurant and even a beer museum.

One end of this plaza is dominated, surprisingly, by what looks like a three-storey brick and stone reproduction of a French chateau. This remarkable structure is a monument to the culinary prowess of France's own Michelin-starred chef Joël Robuchon, the creative force behind each of the four establishments within: a bar, a patisserie and two restaurants. One block beyond the chateau, yet still in the Yebisu Garden Place complex, stands The Westin Tokyo.

Off to one side of the Chateau is the Yebisu Garden Cinema, a theatre specialising in art-house films. Film art of a different kind is displayed at The Tokyo Metropolitan Museum of Photography, which is also part of the complex. A short distance to the south is the Metropolitan Teien Museum of Art, housed in an Art Deco mansion built in 1933 as the home of an Imperial Prince. Exhibitions change regularly, yet the facility itself is pleasant to explore, with its antique wooden floors, broad staircases, high ceilings and extensive gardens. The Mizuma Art Gallery, which stands on the opposite side of Ebisu, near Nakameguro Station, is a showcase for contemporary Japanese art, where exhibits have highlighted the eccentric eroticism of Makoto Aida and the mildly surreal cityscapes of Akira Yamaguchi.

THIS PAGE (CLOCKWISE FROM TOP):
Bienvenue au Tokyo! This chateau is a little piece of France in Ebisu, complete with Joël Robuchon eateries inside; Kondo, a piece of art from the Mizuma Art Gallery; Chef Joël Robuchon himself.
OPPOSITE (FROM LEFT): Tenmyouya, another artwork at Mizuma; a Roppongi Hills apartment, the epitome of a room with a view.

roppongi + azabu

The name Roppongi literally means 'Six Trees', but timber is not what this neighbourhood inside the Yamanote Line is best known for today. A more up-to-date name might be 'Two Towers'. There are few buildings here over a dozen storeys tall, which made the 54-storey Mori Tower at Roppongi Hills impossible to ignore when it opened in 2003. But then, who would want to ignore it? Roppongi Hills quickly established itself as an important part of Tokyo's cultural life. The tower's upper floors house the Mori Art Museum, the city's highest-profile venue for contemporary art. Its debut show drew a reported 730,000 visitors. Closer to ground level, the complex includes one of Tokyo's most impressive multiplexes, the Virgin Toho Cinemas, which boasts the nation's largest screen. The cinemas serve as a venue for much of the Tokyo International Film Festival, plus numerous high-profile premieres. The complex also includes the Grand Hyatt Tokyo and a choice array of shops, such as the clothing store Y's by designer Yohji Yamamoto, and eateries such as L'Atelier de Joël Robuchon. So instantly recognisable has the tower become, that it—or a building that happens to look exactly like it—appears in Sega's hit video game *Yakuza*.

While the complex has done a great deal to make the already popular Roppongi a more attractive place, it no longer has the sky to itself. The neighbourhood's second tower, part of the Tokyo Midtown complex, opened in 2007. Like Roppongi Hills, Tokyo Midtown includes a top-flight hotel and a major art museum. The Ritz-Carlton, Tokyo occupies the top nine levels of

the 53-storey building, and the Suntory Museum of Art displays its large collection of antique Japanese artworks and craft items closer to the ground. Shops here include a branch of Issey Miyake's Pleats Please and the first Japan outlet of Italian clothier Cruciani. Japan firsts in the restaurant category include Conran and Partners' Botanica and the first Japan branch of New York's famed Union Square Cafe. Tokyo Midtown is also home to a new branch of Roti.

A third building, the National Art Center, Tokyo, forms a triangle with the two new towers. While not nearly as tall, it is of a similar vintage (opened in 2007) and is a spectacular piece of architecture in its own right. Designed by Kisho Kurokawa, its dramatically undulating glass façade lets sunlight flood into a front atrium with a 21.6-m- (71-ft-) high ceiling, beneath which a café and a Paul Bocuse restaurant stand on inverted cone pillars. The vast gallery space is reached from the atrium by entrances at several levels, but it's difficult to predict what you may find there. The National Art Center has no permanent collection of its own. Instead, it hosts an ever-changing array of shows.

Roppongi is partially surrounded by the adjacent Azabu neighbourhoods, which are characterised by genteel residences and a panoply of embassies, including those of France, Germany, Greece and China. There are plenty of fine restaurants scattered among those diplomatic establishments, including the appropriately international French-Japanese restaurant Citabria, in Nishi-Azabu, and the more traditional Japanese, Miyashita, across the street from the Austrian Embassy in Moto-Azabu. Chef Kazuhiko Nishihara builds international fusion cuisine on an Italian foundation at Furutoshi, in Nishi-Azabu, while Furutoshi's sister restaurant Pacific Currents jazzes up Franco-Italian food with various Asian spices in Azabu-Juban, in the direction of Tokyo Tower.

At 333 m (1,092 ft), Tokyo Tower, just to the east of the Roppongi and Azabu areas, was once the predominant feature on the city's skyline, but now it is just one giant among many. Built in 1958 as a platform for radio and television antennas, this Eiffel Tower lookalike is gorgeously illuminated at night—making it a highlight of the view from the Mori Tower or Tokyo Midtown.

THIS PAGE (FROM LEFT): *Waves and cones are the dominant shapes in the design of the National Art Center, Tokyo, opened in 2007; modern art forms part of an exhibition at the Art Center.*

OPPOSITE: *Leading Japanese designer Issey Miyake's 2007 Spring Summer Collection.*

...an important part of Tokyo's cultural life.

Four Seasons Hotel Tokyo at Chinzan-so

THIS PAGE (FROM TOP): In a tranquil setting, Four Seasons Hotel Tokyo at Chinzan-so displays a unique blend of classical European décor and traditional Japanese style; located on the fifth floor, the Conservatory Rooms overlook the gardens.

OPPOSITE (CLOCKWISE FROM LEFT): Enjoy a relaxing cup of afternoon tea or evening cocktail at Le Jardin; at Miyuki, traditional Japanese cuisine is served by staff dressed in kimono; the beautiful city skyline is evident from the guestroom.

Surrounded by a beautifully manicured garden, Four Seasons Hotel Tokyo at Chinzan-so is an exquisite hideaway from the neon lights and bustling streets of Tokyo. A leisurely stroll through the Chinzan-so Gardens will take guests to some of its most beautiful spots. One of the oldest temple structures remaining in Tokyo, the Sanjunoto, or three-storeyed pagoda, is an attraction not to be missed, while the tranquil presence of the historic Shiratama Inari Shrine offers a reassuring sense of serenity from the frenzied world outside. With an old spring well and an array of exotic plants and trees, the peaceful Chinzan-so Gardens are indeed one of the city's most distinguished.

With both indoor and outdoor dining concepts, the hotel houses five outstanding restaurants and bars. The widely acclaimed Il Teatro is famed for its tasty authentic Milanese flavours and extraordinary culinary aesthetics. Just as classy in its décor, Venetian glass chandeliers hang in the panelled dining room of the restaurant.

Beneath a wooden rafted ceiling, the huge arched windows of Miyuki overlook the spectacular gardens. Restaurant staff are dressed immaculately in kimono, while stone carvings and delicate pottery all serve to strengthen the restaurant's visual appeal. In the sushi and grill corner, Miyuki serves traditional Japanese food such as kaiseki and shabu-shabu. For special occasions, Kinsui and Hanare-ya make the perfect venue as they serve traditional stone-grilled kaiseki in the most picturesque of settings. Dining in a cottage in the gardens while listening to the murmur of trickling water, this is a great place to sample some of Japan's finest cuisine.

Apart from breathtaking views of the lush gardens, spacious guestrooms also provide magnificent views of the city skyline. Larger suites are fitted with an extravagant living area, while luxurious bathrooms contain a separate rain shower and oversized bath. The hotel's beautiful range of mahogany furniture and silk cushions gives it an air of opulence.

FACTS

ROOMS	283
EATING	Hanare-ya: Japanese • Il Teatro: Italian • Kinsui: Japanese • Miyuki: Japanese • Seasons Bistro: continontal
DRINK	Le Jardin • Le Marquis
FEATURES	banquet rooms • pool • spa
BUSINESS	business centre
NEARBY	Chinzan-so Gardens • Ikebukuro • Mejiro Station
CONTACT	2-10-8 Sekiguchi, Bunkyo-ku, Tokyo, 112-8667 • telephone: +81.3.3943 2222 • facsimile: +81.3.3943 2300 • email: tokyo.concierge@fourseasons.com • website: www.fourseasons.com/tokyo

PHOTOGRAPHS COURTESY OF FOUR SEASONS HOTEL TOKYO AT CHINZAN-SO.

Grand Hyatt Tokyo

With the most expensive real estate in the world and the continual emphasis on the building of 'cities within the city', location is everything in Tokyo. Grand Hyatt Tokyo, the exclusive 'lifestyle destination hotel' in the heart of Roppongi Hills, has found the perfect spot. Japan's largest and most ambitious redevelopment centre boasts over 200 designer shops and numerous restaurants that range from haute cuisine to street cafes. Not forgetting leisure, entertainment and culture, the centre also houses a cinema complex, the Mori Arts Center and landscaped gardens beautifully manicured with waterfalls and ponds. With a subway station connecting Tokyo's fashion hub to the rest of the sights and attractions, it is difficult to avoid Roppongi Hills.

Like its avant-garde surroundings, the hotel combines stunning and dramatic design with luxurious indulgences. The grand lobby emanates an impressive aura with its dark and rich tones, as spotlights glow against warm copper and reflect the highly polished dark flooring. Retro leather chairs are grouped together and around them, giant abstract paintings and prominent sculptures by Jun Kaneko create a modern and exciting ambience.

In a calmer setting, guestrooms are decorated with contemporary, earthy tones and the colours of the natural woods form a tranquil sanctuary. The latest technologies are all in place with a plasma TV, DVD and CD player fitted snugly into each room. The ultimate luxuries, however, are found in the bathrooms. Inspired by the age-old Japanese philosophy behind bathing—an important ritual in daily life—Grand Hyatt Tokyo has created a spectacular environment for cleansing and calming the mind. A huge limestone bath, when filled to the brim with

THIS PAGE (CLOCKWISE FROM TOP): The hotel's style is evident in the grand lobby's décor; combining Western and Japanese elements, the Grand Chapel is an ideal venue for a memorable wedding ceremony; Jun Kaneko's avant-garde sculptures embody the kind of sophistication the hotel exudes.

OPPOSITE: The lavish Presidential Suite provides maximum comfort and indulgence.

...combines stunning and dramatic design with luxurious indulgences.

hot water and fragrant bath oils, flows into a separate basin that surrounds it. With a second television screen in the bathroom, it is possible to sit back, relax and enjoy a film or two while soaking and relaxing in the invigorating essential oils.

For the ultimate indulgence, the Presidential Suite fits the bill. Occupying the entire 21st floor, guests can relax by their private 12-m- (39-ft-) outdoor swimming pool while enjoying a sweeping view of the city, a privilege that only Grand Hyatt Tokyo offers. With the bathroom fitted with a jetted spa tub and rain shower, the suite certainly leaves a lasting impression.

Guests can gain access to the NAGOMI Spa and Fitness for a token sum, while there is also a wide range of cuisines to choose from at the hotel. Be it steak or sushi, al fresco or incognito, the restaurants at Grand Hyatt Tokyo—ranked among the city's best—will not disappoint as they cater to every palate.

FACTS		
	ROOMS	389
	FOOD	Fiorentina: Italian • The French Kitchen Brasserie & Bar: French • Shunbou: Japanese • Roku Roku: sushi • The Oak Door: steakhouse • Chinaroom: Chinese
	DRINK	Maduro
	FEATURES	chapel • spa • fitness centre • pool • function rooms • luxurious bathrooms with rain shower • concierge accredited by Les Clefs D'Or • exclusive amenities
	BUSINESS	business centre • laptop and mobile phone rental
	NEARBY	Roppongi Hills • Roppongi Station • Ginza • Kasumigaseki District
	CONTACT	6-10-3 Roppongi, Minato-ku, Tokyo, 106-0032 • telephone: +81.3.4333 1234 • facsimile: +81.3.4333 8123 • email: info@tyogh.com • website: www.tokyo.grand.hyatt.com

PHOTOGRAPHS COURTESY OF GRAND HYATT TOKYO.

The Ritz-Carlton, Tokyo

THIS PAGE (FROM TOP): Take in the breathtaking city skyline from Tokyo's tallest building; enjoy a swim within the cosy confines of the indoor pool.

OPPOSITE (FROM LEFT): The lobby's avant-garde décor embodies the sophisticated and stylish qualities of the hotel; with excellent amenities and a luxurious interior, guestrooms offer a comfortable stay.

Opened in March 2007, The Ritz-Carlton, Tokyo is as luxurious as its impressive address implies. Situated right in the heart of the Roppongi district, it occupies the first three levels and the top nine floors of a dramatic skyscraper, the sparkling new 53-storey Midtown Tower. Housed in the city's tallest building, the hotel shares access to some excellent facilities, including direct links to three subway lines, the Suntory Museum of Art and a high-end shopping mall in Tokyo Midtown complex.

Surrounded by a beautiful landscape of ponds and cultivated gardens, the hotel is peacefully protected from the constant bustle of Roppongi life. Yet its central location in the city's diplomatic and entertainment hub means that one of Tokyo's most important business districts and numerous restaurants and bars are only a walking distance away. Guests—businessmen in particular—will appreciate the convenience. Leisure travellers can find plenty of attractions that are just as accessible, including the Tokyo Tower, the Imperial Palace and its tranquil gardens. For a sense of Japanese history, guests can visit Sensoji Temple, Tokyo's oldest temple that is one magnificent vermilion-lacquered complex.

As expected from a brand new hotel in Tokyo, the guestrooms are equipped with state-of-the-art facilities such as wireless high-speed Internet access, wi-fi phones and DVD players. Homely comfort is ensured with Frette linens and feather beds. If there is no time for some spa indulgence, the bathrooms—complete with a separate rain shower and double sinks—are stocked with Bvlgari amenities. Should city-break fatigue call for some aided relaxation, The Ritz-Carlton Spa & Fitness will provide the ultimate relief. Designed to take full advantage of the magnificent views from its remarkable position in the sky, it has nine treatment rooms and one spa suite that will provide guests with the best form of relaxing therapies. Alongside the steam and sauna rooms, the rain showers and deep-soaking baths offer pure indulgence. For the health conscious, the hotel's complimentary access to its indoor pool and fitness studio will be very much welcomed.

Roppongi, famed for its energetic nightlife, is a hotspot for young Japanese and expatriates alike. Strolling down Roppongi-dori, guests will be captivated by the amazing array of dining experiences, from the exclusivity of sophisticated sake bars to the excitement of neon-lit diners. Not to be outdone, the hotel has its own stylish Japanese restaurant. With a panoramic view of Mount Fuji, Hinokizaka serves authentic Japanese food complete with teppanyaki, tempura and sushi counters. There is also Forty Five, which offers international cuisine, with Tokyo Tower forming its backdrop. Just as spectacular is The Lobby Lounge & Bar, where a drink at the highest vantage point in Tokyo is rewarded by stunning views of a city awash with neon lights.

FACTS		
ROOMS	248	
FOOD	Forty Five: international • Hinokizaka: Japanese • Café & Deli: patisserie • The Lobby Lounge & Bar: afternoon tea	
DRINK	The Lobby Lounge & Bar • Labels	
FEATURES	The Ritz-Carlton Spa & Fitness • ballroom • banquet area • wedding chapel • business centre	
NEARBY	Roppongi • Kasumigaseki • Marunouchi • Otemachi • Omotesando • Shibuya • Shinjuku	
CONTACT	Tokyo Midtown, 9-7-1 Akasaka, Minato-ku, Tokyo, 107-6245 • telephone: +81.3.3423 8000 • facsimile: +81.3.3423 8001 • website: www.ritzcarlton.com	

PHOTOGRAPHS COURTESY OF THE RITZ-CARLTON, TOKYO.

The Westin Tokyo

Surrounded by open skies and complete with a brilliant view of the nearby Botanical Gardens, The Westin Tokyo offers a luxury rarely found in the city—peace and tranquillity. Located in the vibrant Yebisu Garden Place, a landscaped complex of shops and offices in Ebisu, it is the perfect venue for both work and pleasure. Despite its location in the city centre, Ebisu nonetheless has a rural feel with its steep and narrow lanes. A covered walkway from the hotel also leads directly to the station where Shibuya is just one stop away. Famed for its neon signs, giant video screens and flashing advertisements, the bright lights of Shibuya are one attraction not to be missed.

The hotel lobby exudes European sophistication with its magnificent marble columns, shimmering black marble flooring and stunning neoclassical features. Overlooking the Tokyo Tower and Rainbow

Bridge, the guestrooms are simple yet stylish in décor. With beautifully high ceilings, large windows and spacious living areas, some rooms even come with their own exercise equipment. Cream marble tiling and sparkling glass add a touch of class to the bathrooms. A rain shower and oversized bath also provide a rejuvenating experience, while the hotel's renowned 'Heavenly' bed certainly lives up to its name.

The Westin Tokyo's exceptionally high standard of service is perhaps unsurprising in Japan, a country known for its etiquette, and the hotel's unique facilities only make for an even more comfortable and enjoyable stay. At the push of the 'service express' button, almost anything can be ordered as room service, and guests can even ask to check out over the phone.

THIS PAGE (CLOCKWISE FROM TOP): Enjoy fine Cantonese cuisine in Ryutenmon, the hotel's famous Chinese restaurant; light colour tones give a relaxed feel to the stylish suites; with its neoclassical features, the hotel lobby exudes class and sophistication.

OPPOSITE: Relax in the traditional ambience of Mai, and enjoy its fine Japanese cuisine at the same time.

...offers a luxury rarely found in the city—peace and tranquillity.

With eight restaurants and bars, The Westin Tokyo offers a wide range of styles and flavours, from settings as casual as a café to one as grand and formal as the magnificent Victor's. The view alone on the 22nd floor is worth the trip, particularly at sunset when the Tokyo Tower is magically silhouetted against the deep orange sky. Divided into six areas each with its own theme and mood, Victor's serves innovative Continental cuisine alongside an extensive collection of wines from around the world.

Serving the finest grade of seafood and Kobe beef, Yebisu is a lively teppanyaki restaurant where guests can watch the chef whip up tantalising cuts of meats. A second Japanese restaurant, Mai, is a feast for the eyes in its traditional setting complete with cherry blossoms and frosted glass windows.

For an after dinner drink, The Compass Rose is ideal. There is live music from artistes such as the popular Mississippi pianist-vocalist, Ora Reed.

FACTS		
	ROOMS	438
	FOOD	Mai: Japanese • Ryutenmon: Cantonese • The Terrace: international buffet • Victor's: continental • Yebisu: Japanese
	DRINK	The Bar • The Compass Rose • The Lounge
	FEATURES	beauty salon • executive lounge • fitness club • jogging path • wedding facilities
	BUSINESS	business centre • computer and mobile phone rental
	NEARBY	Botanical Gardens • Ebisu • Meiji Shrine • Roppongi Hills • Shibuya
	CONTACT	1-4-1 Mita, Meguro-ku, Tokyo, 153-8580 • telephone: +81.3.5423 7000 • facsimile: +81.3.5423 7600 • email: wetok@westin.com • website: www.westin.com

PHOTOGRAPHS COURTESY OF THE WESTIN TOKYO.

Citabria

Tucked away on a tiny lane opposite the Chokokuji temple in the residential area of Aoyama, Citabria has become a well-known and well-loved name within Tokyo's fine dining scene.

Entering through a hidden garden where water trickles into a tranquil lily pond, guests are guided to the main dining area by a candlelit path and stairway. Inside, the amber glow creates a warm hideaway, allowing the oriental screens to blend subtly into the wooden and brick background. On one side, there is an inviting bar with a wine cellar that stocks a fine selection of French and Californian wines, while a separate cigar lounge overlooks the tropical entrance through its windows. The leather sofas occupy a comfortable seating area where guests can enjoy some drinks after dinner and indulge in the excellent Cuban cigars.

With Japanese style running through its French décor, Citabria combines the best from the East and West. It attracts both the local and international crowd; even the staff look Parisian chic. Business meetings or celebratory events are well catered for with an exclusive and private dining area. In this luxury private dining suite, there is a lounge area with reclining wicker sofas, personal stereo, a large dining table and a Chef's table offering front row seats to Citabria's main attraction—its food.

Serving modern French cuisine that is influenced by Asian elements, Citabria's fusion fare is light, sumptuous and beautifully presented. The menu, which is divided into sections that are titled 'backyard', 'countryside' and 'seaside', contains an impressive selection of dishes from caviar and foie gras to home-brewed chicken soup. Refreshing starters such as Peach Gazpacho with Chilled Flavours of Peach, Basil and Cucumber or the Beetroot Salad with Feta

Cheese, Candied Nuts and Fig Balsamic offer zesty, aromatic flavours. With a Japanese twist, Citabria has unique dishes such as the Duck Confit with Enoki Mushrooms and Quail stuffed with Lobster Tail. The dessert menu is made up of Western favourites including rhubarb sorbet, and tiramisu, not to mention the restaurant's fine selection of perfectly-matured and melt-in-your-mouth French cheeses.

Like its cuisine, Citabria boasts a simple yet stylish interior that completes the ideal dining experience. With its wooden finishing and a diligent team of staff who provide an impeccable service, diners will enjoy their food in a cosy ambience. Now, guests can have Citabria's intriguing menu customised. Be it family gatherings or business functions, the restaurant's catering service will prepare a special menu to suit the occasion.

OPPOSITE (FROM LEFT): Citabria's décor combines Japanese charm with French style; sample French cuisine in a sophisticated setting.

THIS PAGE (FROM LEFT): The sommelier will pair the perfect bottle of wine with guests' meals; indulge in the luxurious facilities of the private dining suite.

FACTS

SEATS	60
FOOD	modern French
DRINK	cigar lounge • extensive wine list • wine bar
FEATURES	customised menus • vegetarian options
NEARBY	Aoyama • Omotesando • Roppongi • Shibuya
CONTACT	2-26-4 Nishi-Azabu, Minato-ku, Tokyo, 106-0031 • telephone: +81.3.5766 9500 • facsimile: +81.3.5766 9501 • email: info@citabria.co.jp • website: www.citabria.co.jp

PHOTOGRAPHS COURTESY OF CITABRIA.

Den Aquaroom Aoyama

As night falls on the bustling metropolis of Tokyo, the city becomes an ocean of multicoloured gems that sparkle gloriously against the darkened skyline. And when dusk sets in, both the salarymen and their female counterparts, who are known as 'office ladies' in Japan, head for the numerous bars and restaurants in the capital to let their hair down.

One popular district is the centrally located Aoyama. A fashionable part of the city that is frequented by the elite crowd of Tokyo, Aoyama houses Den Aquaroom Aoyama on the quaint street of Kotto-dori. Otherwise known as Antique Street where many renowned boutiques are located, its charming and colourful character makes it a haven for those seeking an alternate yet equally sophisticated hideaway among the many choices that are available in the city.

Descending the stairs of this dining-bar-lounge, visitors are greeted by a stunning interior. Red plush dining chairs and dark wood furnishings make up a stylish décor. But the real star attraction is, undoubtedly, Den Aquaroom Aoyama's breathtaking floor-to-ceiling aquariums.

The enormous fish tanks that decorate the restaurant are impressive, but it is the main aquarium—at 6 m (20 ft) tall—that catches the eye. Created with the deep sea in mind, tropical fish swim about freely as if enticing guests to join them for a casual dip. Relaxing it certainly is, as watching them proves therapeutic for the tired mind.

Den Aquaroom Aoyama has been designed with an emphasis on detail and a sophisticated Balinese flavour. The avant-garde ornaments that adorn the interior

THIS PAGE (CLOCKWISE FROM TOP): **With its soft lighting, the lounge welcomes guests seeking to indulge in a drink or two; the comfortable red chairs enhance Den Aquaroom Aoyama's cosy ambience; enjoy some personal space in the private dining room.** *OPPOSITE:* **The magnificent aquarium makes great company for a relaxing meal.**

blend seamlessly with its classic furniture. The warm light created by the flickering candles and the blue glow of the aquarium offer a cosy atmosphere and the ideal escape from the frenetic pace of city life. Such a unique combination evokes a feel of the sublime and creates a peaceful ambience, not unlike the experience of relaxing under a starlit sky on a breezy evening with a glass of wine in hand.

To counter hunger strikes, look no further than Den Aquaroom Aoyama's menu, which offers an excellent range of authentically prepared French cuisine. Diners will enjoy their meals as dishes are stylishly served and prepared with only the best ingredients.

Regardless of the occasion, any visit—be it for an aperitif, or to wine and dine with friends—to Den Aquaroom Aoyama promises to be a memorable one. Sampling its food and drinks while basking in the soft blue light of the aquarium will re-define the whole dine and wine experience.

FACTS		
	SEATS	69
	FOOD	French-based European cuisine
	DRINKS	wine list • cocktails
	FEATURES	aquariums • excellent quality of food and drinks
	NEARBY	Omotesando Hills • Roppongi Hills
	CONTACT	B1 FIK Minami-Aoyama Building, 5-13-3 Minami-Aoyama, Minato-ku, Tokyo, 107-0062 • telephone: +81.3.5778 2090 • facsimile: +81.3.5778 2096 • email: aqua.aoyama@my.sgn.ne.jp • website: www.myuplanning.co.jp

Furutoshi

Numerous restaurants and bars enliven the picturesque residential district of Nishi-Azabu in Minato-ku. Containing a wealth of international and local cuisine, the area attracts a large expatriate community. Nearby, the wild entertainment district of Roppongi and the spectacular development of restaurants, shops, offices and apartments at Roppongi Hills further invigorate this tiny, yet energetic municipality of Tokyo.

In the heart of such a lively community, Furutoshi caters to a stylish crowd. During summer, the open terrace at the restaurant's front is full of buzz as businessmen, shoppers and residents alike make the most of its sunny spot. Inside, an open-plan kitchen—showing chefs making fresh pasta—steals the limelight. Furutoshi's simple art décor, surrounding dark walls and intimate lighting furnish the spacious dining area with a fresh, European feel. Stunning Japanese orchids on display give the interior an Oriental twist, resulting in an intriguing East-West mix.

Created by French-trained Chef Kazuhiko Nishihara, the menu is a dynamic one that fuses the passion of modern Italian cuisine with the flair of French cooking. Freshly-baked breads and delicious homemade pastas have become a speciality at Furutoshi. Yet the restaurant's thriving success is perhaps better attributed to the tantalising and attractively priced four-course dinner specials, where guests are pampered with an extensive selection of appetisers, pastas, mains and desserts. Made of the finest ingredients, every dish

...fuses the passion of modern Italian cuisine with the flair of French cooking.

arrives beautifully presented. With its generous portions, diners will leave the restaurant with all their cravings satisfied.

Although the menu changes regularly, quality is not compromised. Delectable appetisers include Hokkaido Crab Cakes with Lobster Cream Sauce, while meat lovers will be pleased with the succulent Grilled Tsukuba Pork in Rose-Miso Sauce. A refresher course of tangy sorbets will pave the way for excellent pasta dishes such as Orekiette blended with Rosemary, Trippa and Root Vegetable soup. One of Furutoshi's attractions is its innovative menu that provides a great variety of choices. Offering the freshest of seafood blended with subtle Japanese tastes, favourite mains include Homard Thermidor with Tomato and Sweet Basil Salsa.

To accompany the many rich flavours throughout the meal, Furutoshi's extensive and carefully chosen wine list will not disappoint. There is a range of impressive vintages such as Mouton-Rothschild, as well as an equally fine selection of wines from Italy, France and the US. For those wishing for some quiet and personal space, the restaurant's private rooms are perfect. Like cosmopolitan Tokyo, Furutoshi's fusion fare, coupled with its large bar and impeccable service, makes it the ideal restaurant to indulge in some stylish and sophisticated dining.

PHOTOGRAPHS COURTESY OF FURUTOSHI + VINCENT SUNG.

FACTS		
SEATS	65	
FOOD	European	
DRINK	cigar bar • cocktails • extensive wine list	
FEATURES	private rooms • terrace	
NEARBY	Ginza • Nishi-Azabu • Roppongi Hills	
CONTACT	1, 2F Park View Nishi-Azabu, 1-15-10 Nishi-Azabu, Minato-ku, Tokyo, 106-0031 • telephone: +81.3.5775 1275 • facsimile: +81.3.5775 1276 • email: info@furutoshi.com • website: www.furutoshi.com	

Grand Hyatt Tokyo Restaurants

Roppongi Hills is Tokyo's most dynamic urban development to date. Housing 11 hectares (28 acres) of retail, entertainment and office space, it is set among some of the most beautifully landscaped gardens and innovative architecture in the city. Right at the heart of Roppongi Hills where Grand Hyatt Tokyo is located, over 200 restaurants are within easy reach. By simply stepping inside the hotel, however, guests will discover Grand Hyatt Tokyo's tantalising treats and spectacular designs in some of the city's most renowned restaurants.

In a modern setting of blonde wood and glass, The French Kitchen Brasserie & Bar contains a lively atmosphere. At one end, the frenetic open kitchen comes alive with the activities of the energetic chefs. On the other side, a bustling outdoor terrace overlooks the crowds of businessmen and tourists as they hurry along Keyakizaka Street. Linking the two ends is a catwalk that spans the centre and is banked by narrow channels of flowing water. A floor-to-ceiling glass wine cellar is home to over 3,000 bottles of wine, which is not only a feast for the eyes, but also the perfect complement with excellent food, be it the sumptuous lobster, succulent veal tenderloin or refreshing green pea soup.

Original paintings by Paul Ching Bor hang on the walls of The Oak Door, which operates in a formal setting, catering to the connoisseur meat lover. With a menu of

THIS PAGE (FROM TOP): The stylish catwalk of The French Kitchen Brasserie & Bar; enjoy personal space and a cosy ambience in The Oak Door's private dining room; The Oak Door offers premium meats and a classy décor.

OPPOSITE (FROM LEFT): Roku Roku's chefs prepare the most delectable sushi; Shunbou's showpiece glass-encased camellia.

premium quality meats prepared in oak wood-burning ovens complemented by a diverse range of sauces, the food is indeed exceptional. Cooked according to preference, the grilled rib eye beef is melt-in-the-mouth delicious and is accompanied by the creamiest of coleslaws.

Specialising in sushi and sashimi, Roku Roku employs only the most skilled chefs who create tasty works of art from tuna, sea urchins and ice-fish. The finest quality seafood is assured as ingredients are selected by 'handpicked artisans' from all over Japan with the best training and skills. The sushi bar provides entertainment as the chefs prepare the exquisite sushi in the lively and open arena. An experience not to be missed, diners would no doubt leave Roku Roku very satisfied.

Shunbou, one of the two Japanese restaurants at the Grand Hyatt Tokyo, is set within an amazing and garden-like environment. The counter, a rough slab of granite, has been polished to perfection, creating a shining appearance while the dramatic feature of camellia that is encased in glass produces a novel work of art. The food is equally inspiring, as the ingredients used are the freshest from the market. Apart from serving authentic traditional Japanese cuisine and traditional à la carte dishes such as kaiseki and kappo, the meticulously set menu also allows one to sample more exotic treats like Japan's famed stone fish.

FACTS

EATING	Fiorentina: Italian • The French Kitchen Brasserie & Bar: French • Shunbou: Japanese • Roku Roku: sushi • The Oak Door: steakhouse • Chinaroom: Chinese
FEATURES	freshly handpicked seasonal ingredients • oak wood-burning ovens • open kitchen
NEARBY	Roppongi Hills • Roppongi Station • Ginza • Kasumigaseki District
CONTACT	Grand Hyatt Tokyo, 6-10-3 Roppongi, Minato-ku, Tokyo, 106-0032 • telephone: +81.3.4333 1234 • facsimile: +81.3.4333 8123 • email: info@tyogh.com • website: www.tokyo.grand.hyatt.com

PHOTOGRAPHS COURTESY OF GRAND HYATT TOKYO.

Kurayamizaka Miyashita Restaurants

Aoyama, Azabu, Omotesando and Marunouchi are prime locations in central Tokyo which the trendy and well-heeled like to frequent. Kurayamizaka Miyashita is one name that is synonymous with these upmarket areas, where its young and enterprising owner, Daisuke Miyashita, operates his four restaurants. To be located in yet another sophisticated part of the city— Roppongi Midtown this time—two new outlets are being mapped out for 2007. Since opening his first restaurant in Azabu in 1995, Miyashita's restaurants have won several plaudits for their excellent array of original gourmet dishes.

A stone path lined with black bamboo leads guests to the stylish interior of the Kurayamizaka Miyashita restaurant at Aoyama. The most high end of the Miyashita group of restaurants, the kaiseki courses that Aoyama serves will appeal to guests who wish to experience fine dining at its best. Here, dishes are meticulously prepared to bring the best out of each ingredient, with a special emphasis on vegetables. With its exquisite décor designed by top international designer Kengo Kuma, the restaurant offers a tranquil and relaxing ambience where delectable food is served with the warmest

THIS PAGE (FROM TOP): Aoyama's sleek counter seats will impress as much as its excellent food; the private room at Aoyama offers fine dining as well as some peace and quiet.

OPPOSITE (FROM LEFT): With a magnificent view of the beautiful city skyline, look forward to a memorable dining experience at Marunouchi; Azabu's avant-garde interior adds to its air of exclusivity; enjoy Omotesando's culinary fusion of yoshoku cuisine in the restaurant's stylish setting.

...have won several plaudits for its excellent array of original gourmet dishes.

hospitality. Small dining rooms are also available for guests who hope for some privacy. Personal space is what they will get, as these exclusive dining rooms provide the perfect setting for a peaceful and enjoyable meal of haute Japanese cuisine prepared by skilful chefs.

Miyashita has gone on to open Yoshoku Miyashita in the avant-garde shopping haven of Omotesando Hills. Following the tradition of yoshoku cuisine, whose origins can be traced back to the Meiji era, this restaurant serves Western dishes infused with traditional Japanese flavours, giving a fascinating mix for the palate that will be intrigued by signature dishes such as the omu-raisu, or rice omelette.

Away from the thronging crowd of the shopping mall, the restaurant at Azabu is located in an exclusive residential area where fine, unique Japanese dishes are served, catering to diners who prefer authentic Japanese cuisine. For guests who want to enjoy the double pleasures of fine dining and breathtaking scenery, Miyashita's restaurant at Marunouchi is the place to go. Located on the 36th floor of the Marunouchi Building, the restaurant offers a stunning view of the city skyline that includes the Imperial Palace, ensuring a memorable dining experience indeed.

Four restaurants. Four different dining concepts, each with its own character. Having earned rave reviews and awarded glowing testimonies, any of the Miyashita restaurants is definitely worth a visit.

FACTS

SEATS	28
FOOD	kaiseki
DRINK	wine list • sake list
FEATURES	private dining
NEARBY	Omotesando • Roppongi • Meiji Jingu Stadium • Akasaka Imperial Grounds • state guest house
CONTACT	2-24-8 Minami-Aoyama, Minato-ku, Tokyo, 107-0062 • telephone/facsimile: +81.3.5785 2431 • email: kmacky@ds-miyashita.jp • website: www.ds-miyashita.jp

PHOTOGRAPHS COURTESY OF KURAYAMIZAKA MIYASHITA.

Pacific Currents

THIS PAGE (FROM TOP): *Soft lighting and a spacious dining room enhance the relaxing ambience; sample the unique flavours of Japanese-Italian fusion cuisine.*

OPPOSITE (FROM LEFT): *The dark red walls and stylish furniture make for a sophisticated décor; with a wide selection of wines and relaxing atmosphere, gatherings of wine connoisseurs are not uncommon here at Pacific Currents.*

Close to the throngs of revellers who party all night in Roppongi, Azabu-Juban has managed to retain a charming village feel in the centre of one of Asia's most dynamic cities. As its tree-lined streets bustle with a mixture of Japanese and Western stores, restaurants and bars, century-old family-run shops thrive alongside the expensive apartments and lively dining scene. Local attractions include the Azabu-Juban hot springs, Zenfukuji Temple and the antique markets. Having said that, what the area is most famous for is 'cool breeze matsuri', Tokyo's largest food festival that graces the tiny cobbled streets of Azabu Juban at the end of August every year. Food lovers will be spoilt for choice as they can either experience local delicacies in tiny tatami dens found along the backstreets or sample cuisines from all over the world in several of the international cafés and restaurants.

Fusing passionate Italian cooking with Japanese style and ingredients, Pacific Currents has something for everyone. The

Fusing passionate Italian cooking with Japanese style and ingredients...

restaurant's mix of European and Oriental influence is apparent from its sleek and stylish décor that offers a calming and sophisticated ambience. Attracting a lively crowd throughout the year, the interior is dominated by the warmth of the deep red walls, comfortable cream leather armchairs and large open windows that overlook Azabu-Juban's tree-lined high street.

In a style similar to its sister restaurants, Furutoshi and Sky, Pacific Currents serves various fusion dishes featuring delicious homemade pastas, the freshest seafood, exotic herbs and spices from around the world and plenty of organic vegetarian options. There is an amazing variety of appetisers alone. Beef Carpaccio with Mimolette Cheese, Mustard and Balsamic Caramel, and Roasted Vegetables with Mascarpone Cheese and Yuzu Vinaigrette are two of the interesting entries on offer.

With the pasta freshly prepared each day, melt-in-the-mouth dishes such as Tagliatelle with Shrimp and Kyoto Taro Ohba cannot be missed. Blending traditional favourites with a Japanese flavour, the main courses at Pacific Currents combine the best ingredients to produce some of the most delicious and creative dishes. Chef's recommendations include a fine assortment. Fillet Beef with Wasabi Sauce, and Lamb Chop in Red Wine and Teriyaki Sauce—just to name two—are both highly popular. The perfect complement to such an excellent menu is the equally impressive wine list. In fact, so good is its collection that wine lovers gather here regularly to indulge in some fine wine. For those so inclined, the cocktail list is just as extensive. To top it off, the polite and professional service at Pacific Currents is second to none. It also offers catering services, wine evenings and private dinners where guests can organise their own business events or celebrations in the restaurant's exclusive private rooms.

FACTS		
SEATS	50	
FOOD	fusion	
DRINK	extensive wine list • new world wine	
FEATURES	catering • private functions • private rooms • wine evenings	
NEARBY	Antiques market • Azabu-Juban • Azabu-Juban hot springs • Ginza • Roppongi Hills • Zenfukuji Temple	
CONTACT	2F Marto Building, 2-20-7 Azabu-Juban, Minato-ku, Tokyo, 106-0045 • telephone: +81.3.5765 2356 • facsimile: +81.3.5765 2357 • email: info@pacificcurrents.com • website: www.pacificcurrents.com	

PHOTOGRAPHS COURTESY OF PACIFIC CURRENTS.

Roti

Roti's speciality lies in its rotisserie chicken. Charbroiled over an open vertical flame, the chicken is immediately seared, which makes it crispy while retaining all the natural goodness. The restaurant also uses its own brand of special olive oil marinades, spice and herb rubs that enhance the taste of their rotisserie dishes. Using the lava rock grill, Roti's tasty chargrilled steaks and seafood are infused with a touch of originality and zest with the marinades and herb rubs. For a healthier alternative to frying, many of the vegetables and appetisers are also grilled.

With more than 20 years of culinary experience in the restaurant scene in Tokyo, London, Los Angeles and San Francisco, the restaurant is in the good hands of Chef Ian

THIS PAGE (FROM TOP): Relax and enjoy Chef Tozer's dynamic dishes in Roti's cosy interior; pick a bottle from the restaurant's extensive wine list to go with its excellent food.

OPPOSITE (FROM LEFT): Roti offers quality grilled meat and fine wines in a stylish setting; regardless of the weather, guests can always enjoy a peaceful meal on the restaurant's patio.

Visiting Japan and sampling local flavours in the traditional tatami-mat setting is a must, but the traveller should be aware that good restaurants serving juicy, roasted meats—Western-style, straight off from the grill—exist as well. Roti is one such place. A modern American brasserie, the restaurant is located next to the stylish Roppongi Hills in central Tokyo.

With a cosy ambience, Roti offers wholesome and home-style cooking.

Philip Tozer. Believing in the concept of simplicity, the free-spirited Briton 'cooks what he likes the way he likes it,' infusing much dynamism into his dishes.

Other tempting salad and pasta dishes on the menu include Roti's Caesar Salad and Ricotta Gnocchi, alongside traditional American desserts like N.Y. Cheesecake and Pecan Pie. Open daily, an all-day breakfast is served on Sundays, which

provides a set menu offering a main course such as Eggs Benedict and Blueberry Pancakes that is well complemented with the cereals, toast and fresh fruits that are served at the self-service counter. Roti does not forget its young patrons either, as children can enjoy a proper Sunday breakfast with selection from the Kids' Menu.

With staff hailing from countries such as England, Israel, Chile and Mexico, the restaurant possesses an impressively international roster. As most of them speak English and are bilingual, guests will be reassured to know that nothing will be lost in translation when they order their food. Rain or shine, diners can look forward to a quiet and relaxing meal outdoors at Roti, for part of the dining area on its large patio—one of the best in Tokyo—is covered. For the wine connoisseur, Roti has a great wine menu featuring blackboard specials of rare wines and more than 60 wines from North America and the New World.

With a cosy ambience, Roti offers wholesome and home-style cooking. If anyone feels a craving for grilled meat in Tokyo, this is the place to keep in mind.

FACTS

SEATS	87
FOOD	modern American
DRINK	cocktails • wine list
FEATURES	chargrilled steaks • rotisserie chicken • Redhook from Seattle • microbrewed ales from Oregon's Rogue Brewery • patio seating
NEARBY	Tokyo Midtown
CONTACT	1F Piramide Building, 6-6-9 Roppongi, Minato-ku, Tokyo 106-0230 • telephone: +81.3.5785 3671 • facsimile: +81.3.5785 3672 • email: info@rotico.com • website: www.rotico.com

Stair

THIS PAGE (FROM TOP): *Stair's stylish décor and equally sophisticated European cuisine complement each other perfectly; be it liqueur or cocktails, guests will find what they want from the wide-ranging wine list.*

OPPOSITE: *Admire the intricacies of the avant-garde designs on the walls and frosted window.*

Situated above the Dresscamp boutique, Stair has been offering European fine dining in the trendy Aoyama district of Tokyo since April 2005. Helping to add a touch of subtlety and contemporary charm to the restaurant is the renowned Masamichi Katayama, the architect behind the design which manages to find perfect harmony with the energy of the bustling city. From young executives to art gurus, visitors lounge here till late into the night to indulge in Stair's cosy ambience as much as its original cuisine.

The highlight of the restaurant is undoubtedly its luxury lounge, which is created with the discerning visitor in mind. Projecting a gorgeous and seductive image, the lounge offers an intriguing blend of style and popular culture. Rosewood finishing

...a luxurious night venue for guests to relax and indulge in.

For a little variation, the menu offers organic dishes as well. The Organic Vegetable Salad with Consommé Gelée is, in fact, one of Stair's popular starters. For meat lovers, there is the Grilled Japanese Fillet and Foie Gras with Red Wine Sauce, or Roast Date Chicken from Fukushima with Artichoke Salad, to satisfy their cravings. With the restaurant opened till as late as 4 am, guests have all the time to relax and enjoy their meal with a drink or two, which can be picked from Stair's impressive wine list.

An interesting facet to the restaurant is a gallery space reserved specially for photographers. A place where the walls are stylishly adorned with photos that are just as sophisticated, photographers are free to contribute to this photo collection that enhances the vibrant feel of the restaurant. Backed by a superb live band, Stair is a treat for the senses, presenting a luxurious night venue for guests to relax and indulge in.

that is accompanied by authentic ornaments like marvel stones creates a sophisticated interior, while the series of abstract and psychedelic paintings—likened to tattoo art in the air—is a worthy addition to Stair's avant-garde décor.

Such dynamic atmosphere is replicated in the kitchen, where Stair's excellent European cuisine is produced. Although the menu changes seasonally, the quality of food remains top class, for only the freshest and finest ingredients are used every time.

FACTS		
	SEATS	50
	FOOD	European
	DRINK	extensive wine list
	FEATURES	luxury lounge with authentic meals • space gallery • live music
	NEARBY	Aoyama • Harajuku • Meiji Shrine • Omotesando • Shibuya • Yoyogi Park
	CONTACT	2F, 5-5-1 Minami-Aoyama, Minato-ku, Tokyo, 107-0062 • telephone: +81.3.5778 3773 • facsimile: +81.3.5778 3773 • email: stair@air.ocn.ne.jp • website: www.stair-lounge.com

PHOTOGRAPHS COURTESY OF AT'ONE CO. LTD.

Super Dining Zipangu

By day, Akasaka is a commercial district powered by company headquarters and foreign embassies as the streets are crowded with salarymen hurrying to and from meetings. The grand Akasaka Palace, located in the commercial heart of the district, is not open to the casual visitor. Rather, this spectacular building is used as a State guesthouse. The Hie Shrine, located at the top of a steep hill and surrounded by beautiful landscaped gardens, attracts more lunchtime office workers than tourists.

At night however, Akasaka abandons its corporate image and parties alongside neighbouring Roppongi. Restaurants and bars line the streets and entice both the international and local crowd, who come to enjoy some upmarket entertainment. In the nearby Akasaka Excel Hotel, Super

Dining Zipangu has recreated the lively atmosphere of its surrounding streets with six separate dining areas and bars. A spacious main dining area with low ceilings and intimate spotlighting has a casual and enjoyable ambience. Predominantly made from blonde wood, from the walls to the tables, the restaurant exudes a rustic charm with its heavy beams. In the centre is a table for 20 people, the ideal setting for large groups. Zipangu also caters for intimate dinners for two, with small circular tables overlooking the stunning views of Shinjuku through full-length windows. These popular prime-position seats are much sought after and early booking is recommended.

Four granite counters, each seating 10, give guests the opportunity to sit up close and personal with their chef. Each counter is

THIS PAGE (CLOCKWISE FROM TOP): The cigar lounge is one unique facility offered by Zipangu; enjoy personal space in the stylish private dining rooms; the comfortable sofas, premium sake, wine and cigars will ensure an enjoyable night.

OPPOSITE: The restaurant's spectacular entrance paves the way for a sophisticated dining experience.

dedicated to a particular style of Japanese cuisine, from the fresh fish counter for sashimi and sushi, to the nimono counter for steaming Japanese stew. There are also the grill and teppanyaki counters that serve yakitori—skewered grilled chicken, steak and charbroiled dishes—as well as the busy sake-tasting counter.

For somewhere with a little more privacy, there are seven semi-private dining rooms, seating between four and 20 guests. Each room is decorated in traditional Japanese style complete with wooden screens and hard granite stone from the Kagawa Prefecture. The sunken kotatsu tables give a cosy and intimate feel for even a large group. After dinner, the cigar lounge is the ideal place to relax with its comfortable red sofas and impressive list of premium sake, wine and cigars.

As part of the Nadaman Group, which is famed for traditional Japanese cuisine across the country, Super Dining Zipangu focuses on the best seasonal flavours and ingredients to serve traditional dishes with a Western twist. Open until 3 am with a late night menu prepared after 11 pm, there is plenty of time for some super dining, Zipangu-style.

PHOTOGRAPHS COURTESY OF NADAMAN SUPER DINING ZIPANGU.

FACTS

SEATS	300
FOOD	Japanese with Western twist
DRINK	cigar lounge • sake counter
FEATURES	extensive wine list
NEARBY	Akasaka • Akasaka Palace • Hie Shrine • Itsunoki-dori • Nagatacho • Roppongi • Shinjuku
CONTACT	14F Akasaka Excel Hotel, 2-14-3 Nagatacho, Chiyoda-ku, Tokyo, 100-0014 • telephone: +81.3.3580 3661 • facsimile: +81.3.3589 3112 • email: zipangu@nadaman.co.jp • website: www.nadaman.co.jp

Badou-R

THIS PAGE (FROM TOP): *45rpm is renowned for its denim and indigo-dyed line of clothing; Badou-R's wooden décor complements the adventurous spirit of its products.*

OPPOSITE (FROM LEFT): *A wide range of stoles and other indigo-dyed accessories is available; take a walk back in time while shopping within the rustic premises of Badou-R.*

Although it is named after the traditional analogue vinyl disc, or gramophone record, Japan's 45rpm has nothing to do with music production. Incorporated in 1977, 45rpm is a clothing company which, like its namesake, hopes to become a source of original and exciting non-stop hits, or clothes, in this case.

45rpm has become well-known for its quality denim and indigo-dyed products, and in true Japanese fashion, much attention has been paid to detail. Everything, from the cut and craftsmanship to the dyes of the fabric, is taken care of. After experimenting with different types of dyes, 45rpm finally came up with its famous 'Japan Blue' indigo that is based on the dyes used to colour the clothing of Japanese farmers.

It is such constant innovation and effort to produce only the best that led 45rpm to set up Badou-R, its flagship store in Tokyo, in 1999. Located in the quiet residential neighbourhood of Minami-Aoyama—a luxury shopping district of the city—this shop is housed in a beautiful traditional Japanese home, the perfect setting for its classic 'made-in-Japan' line of clothing. Holding firm to the belief of 'materials first', which places the importance of selecting the best materials above everything else, Badou-R's clothing is undoubtedly of the finest quality. Here, shopping is a relaxing affair. As the Japanese do at home, visitors take off their shoes before entering the shop, while the beautiful surrounding greenery adds to the charm of the place.

...well-known for its quality denim and indigo-dyed products...

Inspired by techniques used in the traditional handicraft world—India and Vietnam come to mind—Badou-R produces clothing with an earthy theme, combining them with denim to create a bold yet rugged and stylish contrast. The denim sold here is dyed using the traditional ai, or Japanese plant indigo dye, which has been fused with American denim. In the shop, there is a fine selection on display. Ranging from inner blouses to scarves and stoles, including all the other indigo-dyed products, visitors will certainly not leave empty-handed.

Apart from its own brand name, Badou-R also carries a collection from its umii908 line. This collection strives to extract the best of the bold and dynamic seafaring cultures from countries such as France and Hawaii. In fact, 'umii' means ocean or sea in Japanese. Again, quality is emphasised as only the best raw materials are used to produce this line of clothing. A rare material, Suvin cotton, which represents only two to three per cent of the quantity of cotton produced in the world, is mostly used for umii products. Another material used is

hemp, which is dyed using Badou-R's famous indigo dye, giving the clothes an antiquated look.

With an intriguing mix of east and west, and old and new, 45rpm's Badou-R is one unique store in central Tokyo that will entice any discerning shopper to step right inside this Japanese home.

FACTS

PRODUCTS	clothing • stoles • bandanas • hats • accessories • belts • shoes
FEATURES	indigo-dyed products • denim • handmade clothing • shop in a relaxing atmosphere over tea
NEARBY	Aoyama Kotto-dori • Nezu Museum
CONTACT	7-7-21 Minami-Aoyama, Minato-ku, Tokyo, 107-0062 • telephone: +81.3.5778 0045 • facsimile: +81.3.3498 9945 • email: shop-badour@45rpm.co.jp • website: www.45rpm.jp

PHOTOGRAPHS COURTESY OF 45RPM STUDIO CO. LTD.

Dresscamp

Based in Tokyo, the Dresscamp label possesses a unique mix which sees classical elements blended seamlessly with modern ideas. Both of its men's and women's collections consist of original print materials that are intricately decorated with Swarovski Crystals in an innovative fashion.

In January 2005, Iwaya opened Dresscamp's flagship store in Tokyo's prestigious Aoyama district, where many renowned boutiques and popular fine dining restaurants reside. Designed by Masamichi Katayama, the store's stylish interior boasts breathtaking Swarovski Crystal chandeliers, alongside the three magnificent lion statues. There is also a splendid mirror display and a video screen on the wall that form part of the store's sophisticated décor.

THIS PAGE (FROM TOP): The store's three lion statues embody the fiery and dynamic spirit of the Dresscamp brand; the men's collection mixes style with stunning designs.
OPPOSITE: The women's collection is just as eye catching.

Since its sensational debut at Tokyo Collection in 2002, Dresscamp has gone from strength to strength, emerging as one of the most innovative fashion brands in Japan today. Led by designer Toshikazu Iwaya, who was awarded Best Newcomer at the 2004 Mainichi Fashion Awards, Dresscamp's line of clothing exudes glamour and a sense of novelty, attracting a loyal following among fashionistas.

...exudes glamour and a sense of novelty, attracting a loyal following among fashionistas.

On the original print materials of each of the women's and men's collection is a specific theme that kickstarts the entire design process. An idea is first drawn, before a method of printing is chosen accordingly, which includes dyeing and using silk screen among others. Dresscamp's dresses and accessories are tailored for fashionable individuals who like their clothes with a distinct style and identity. To Dresscamp, craftsmanship and passion for materials have an important role to play in the whole creation process to achieve the elusive brand concept. This is evident in its range of clothing at its Aoyama store, as well as other outlets in Japan and abroad. Today, Dresscamp enjoys many collaborations with renowned brands such as Duvetica, Peal Izumi, Hirata Akio, Oliver Goldsmith and others. On his own, Iwaya has also participated in various design engagements with Piaget and Viva You, testimony to Dresscamp's growing stature in the fashion world.

FACTS

PRODUCTS	clothing • accessories
FEATURES	decorative and modern designs
NEARBY	Aoyama • Omotesando • Shibuya • Harajuku • Yoyogi Park • Meiji Shrine
CONTACT	2-33-12-503 Jingumae, Shibuya-ku, Tokyo, 150-0001 • telephone: +81.3.3423 1279 • facsimile: +81.3.3423 0826 • email: info@dresscamp.org • website: www.dresscamp.org

PHOTOGRAPHS COURTESY OF AT'ONE CO. LTD.

Fuji-Torii

Much has changed since Fuji-Torii opened its doors along Omotesando Road in 1949. Despite being surrounded by some of the world's most prestigious brands today, Fuji-Torii has managed to retain its century-old tradition as a family-run antiques dealer. Indeed, Fuji-Torii's old-world charm forms a fascinating contrast to the international outlook and exuberance of its neighbours, which include Tokyo's newest fashion and entertainment complexes and the city's most radical teenage gathering points along the famed Takeshita Street.

First established as a small shop in the Asakusa district by Kakujiro Kurihara, Fuji-Torii has passed through three generations and is now managed by the grandson, Naohiro Kurihara. With a hundred years of

THIS PAGE (FROM TOP): An intricately-designed porcelain plate; a beautiful lacquer Suzuribako box set with plum blossom and willow motifs, handmade by Hobi Uematu.

OPPOSITE (FROM LEFT): Fuji-Torii's excellent range of antiques; the ancient Japanese warrior embodies the shop's classical yet sophisticated style; exquisite vases on display.

experience in the trade, the Kurihara family possesses an intimate knowledge of Japan's antiques, from traditional silk paintings to samurai swords. Resembling a refined Japanese home with artwork and scrolls on the walls, the showroom also has cabinets, tables and sofas tucked snugly around the shop floor. With an ever broadening selection of goods and a workshop of their own, Fuji-Torii now designs, produces and sells modern handicrafts and Japanese stationery alongside its impressive collection of antiques and traditional art and craft work.

Both modern designs and restored antiques have been carefully selected and looked after to ensure quality merchandise. Traditional Japanese screens and silk scrolls, hand-painted and signed by professional artists, express the beauty of the four seasons with cherry blossom motifs and snow-covered landscapes. Stunning lacquerware,

having endured months of labour-intensive work, feature complex and layered designs. With this ancient art fast becoming a sunset industry as fewer and fewer apprentices dedicate themselves to learning a skill that requires so much patience, these old Japanese pieces, such as the exquisite 18th-century boxes at Fuji-Torii, are becoming increasingly rare and precious.

Metal craft remains highly regarded in Japan and bronze work, in the form of sculptures and vases, is displayed in Fuji-Torii. The intricate baskets are made from bamboo, its dense and flexible texture allowing it to be shaped into unusual yet sturdy weavings. Focusing on traditional designs, Fuji-Torii collects and makes all kinds of porcelain, from bowls and vases to teacups and sake jars. Numerous styles that portray Japan's long history can be found in the shop, including Imari, which dates back more than 400 years. There is the Satsuma style, defined by its highly decorated designs and gold outlines, and the Kutani motif, which has highly individualistic and simple designs with a colour combination of blue, green, purple, yellow and red.

Ranging from products for everyday use to fine artwork, Fuji-Torii's diverse collection has attracted regular visits from foreigners and locals alike, including Japanese diplomats searching for national mementos for their counterparts overseas. It is no surprise then that Naohiro Kurihara's collectibles can be found in many famous hallways outside of Japan.

FACTS

PRODUCTS traditional Japanese antiques • home decorations • art and craft
FEATURES showroom and warehouse • overseas shipping and delivery
NEARBY Harajuku • Meiji Shrine • Omotesando Hills • Takeshita Street
CONTACT 6-1-10 Jingumae, Shibuya-ku, Tokyo, 150-0001 •
telephone: +81.3.3400 2777 • facsimile: +81.3.3400 5777 •
website: www.fuji-torii.com

PHOTOGRAPHS COURTESY OF FUJI-TORII + TAKERU.

Issey Miyake Aoyama

THIS PAGE (FROM TOP): *The dazzling vibrancy and avant-garde interior of the fashion gallery; Issey Miyake offers nothing less than style and sophistication.*

OPPOSITE: *Its creative designs and style have made Issey Miyake a household name in the international world of fashion.*

Home to the most exclusive boutiques, the tiny neighbourhood of Aoyama and Omotesando remains the ultimate location for the latest designer fashion. Drawing Tokyo's fashionistas, this is where world-renowned designers house their flagship stores. Nearby, Harajuku attracts a different crowd, being a favourite hangout for radical teens dressed in dramatic cos-play costumes. Together they make up the city's famous shopping district, and a fascinating destination for visitors to explore.

Issey Miyake's stunning fashion gallery conveys the innovative vision of its brand. The shop stands out from the others on the street. Here, everything is bold, from the soft white walls to the contrasting stone flooring, along with its brilliant and unconventional clothing designs. Most of Issey Miyake's collections are inspired by technology and constant experimentation. The flagship store is always updated with interactive displays, and is recognised as a dynamic gallery of art as much as a gallery of fashion.

...Issey Miyake's collections are inspired by technology and constant experimentation.

With a number of boutiques in Tokyo, New York, London and Paris, Issey Miyake is revered today as one of the industry's most influential fashion designers. In 2007, Dai Fujiwara took over as Creative Director and has continued to create the distinctive designs that define Issey Miyake. Through research and development, fabrics and creations range from suits that are handmade from natural materials to avant-garde dresses made from synthetic fabrics.

The unique designs cater to every occasion, from casual wear to sophisticated work and evening attire.

With the designs so well received by Tokyo's discerning shoppers, it is not surprising to see the launch of another brand under the Issey Miyake line. Drawing from the same innovative vision that has made Issey Miyake a household name, the Fête collection caters specifically to women, and is characterised by its unusual yet dynamic

colour combination, befitting its namesake, which means 'celebration' in French. And as Issey Miyake continues to expand worldwide as well as regionally, a new flagship store was opened in Osaka recently. It houses all collections under the Issey Miyake umbrella, as well as other selected brands. With its extensive international exposure, Issey Miyake's avant-garde design is a must for the complete shopping experience in Tokyo.

FACTS

PRODUCTS	clothing • accessories
FEATURES	stunning shop floor • dynamic and bold designs • various Issey Miyake labels
NEARBY	Aoyama • Harajuku • Meiji Shrine • Omotesando • Shibuya • Yoyogi Park
CONTACT	3-18-11 Minami-Aoyama, Minato-ku, Tokyo, 107-0062
	telephone: +81.3.3423 1408 • website: www.isseymiyake.com

PHOTOGRAPHS COURTESY OF ISSEY MIYAKE INC.

Mizuma Art Gallery

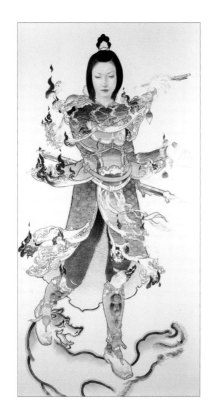

Mizuma Art Gallery is leading a new trend in Japanese art, dictated by the young and fearless new generation. Shaped by a sense of community and the dynamism of diversity, this unique and cultural-savvy generation strives to be different from its predecessors. Their experimentation with new ideas and radical portrayals of traditional values have paved the way for a new and controversial style in the arts. Owner Sueo Mitsuma, inspired by the ideal to introduce these fascinating works of art to collectors all over the globe, established Mizuma Art Gallery in 1994. Today, it is regarded as the fundamental channel between Japan's new generation of artists and its contemporaries from around the world.

Located in the hub of Tokyo's young and fashionable district—close to the bustling, neon streets of Shibuya, the radical gatherings in Harajuku and the wild parties in Roppongi—Mizuma Art Gallery sits on the pulse of Japan's future. Frequently

THIS PAGE (CLOCKWISE FROM TOP): 'Shitenno Komokuten' or 'Four Heavenly Kings', a watercolour art by Akira Yamaguchi; one of the captivating works on display, 'Giant Salamander' by Makoto Aida, 2003; Hisashi Tenmyouya's acrylic piece, 'Japanese Spirit #1'.

OPPOSITE (FROM LEFT): Tomoko Konoike paints an air of mystery in 'The Planet is Covered by Silvery Sleep'; Koji Tanada's 'Sea Horizon, Girl E', painted on wood.

Educated in the US and now residing in Ho Chi Minh City, Vietnam, Jun Nguyen-Hatsushiba is most famous for his beautiful underwater photography and videos. Combining rickshaws and fishermen, he produces authenticity by injecting a sense of political realism into his subjects. Makoto Aida, arguably Japan's greatest living artist, has gained international renown as a painter, sculptor, novelist and manga artist. His works cover a huge range, such as nihon-ga (traditional Japanese painting) and oil painting, all of which have been shown in several solo and group exhibitions. Works of Hirofu Iso, otherwise known as Komainu, have been exhibited in Paris and comprise abstract positions of everyday furniture, from pot plants hanging from the ceiling to computer-like boxes that are seemingly floating in space. Other artists represented by Mizuma Art Gallery include Akira Yamaguchi, Hisashi Tenmyouya, Tomoko Konoike and Hiroko Okada.

For serious collectors or casual enquirers interested in this new era of Japanese art, Mizuma Art Gallery captures a fascinating insight to the thoughts, imagination and beliefs of a subculture that is set to become the future of Japan. Already turning heads throughout Japan and around the world with its creations, it is a generation that Mizuma is careful not to neglect.

representing its diverse group of artists at fairs from Miami to Melbourne and Venice to Istanbul, Mizuma is fast attracting the attention of the international art community and a significant number of collectors.

Mizuma Art Gallery currently represents 26 artists and is host to several solo and group exhibitions. Its featured works are highly diverse and controversial, created by some of Japan's most prominent artists.

FACTS

PRODUCTS	contemporary art
FEATURES	26 prominent young Japanese artists represented • frequent exhibitions
NEARBY	Ebisu • Harajuku • Meguro • Roppongi • Shibuya
CONTACT	2F Fujiya Building, 1-3-9 Kamimeguro, Meguro-ku, Tokyo, 153-0051 • telephone: +81.3.3793 7931 • facsimile: +81.3.3793 7887 • email: gallery@mizuma-art.co.jp • website: www.mizuma-art.co.jp

PHOTOGRAPHS COURTESY OF MIZUMA ART GALLERY.

Omotesando Hills

One stop away on the JR line from the shopping and entertainment district of Shibuya is Harajuku, which lies in the Aoyama district to the southwest of Tokyo. A haven for Japan's trendy youth, the famous lanes surrounding Takeshita Street are crowded with teenagers and lined with fast food restaurants and shops selling the latest fashion wear. On Sundays, the area becomes a showcase for cos-play, as youths throng the streets decked out in the most outlandish outfits, recreating the gothic look or imitating anime characters. Spilling onto

THIS PAGE (FROM TOP): *The style and sophistication of this shopping haven will appeal to the trendy and fashion-conscious; be dazzled by the scintillating lights and colours at night.* OPPOSITE: *Experience superb shopping, excellent food and an amazing atmosphere, all under one roof.*

the nearby Yoyogi Park and Meiji Shrine, these youngsters, with their infectious energy, create a fascinating sight.

Linking this sophisticated neighbourhood to Aoyama-dori and Omotesando Station is Omotesando boulevard, an equally intriguing fashion hub. Here, famous international brands line the streets, offering the latest and most stylish designer wear and accessories. Known as the Champs-Élysées of Tokyo, it is not uncommon to see queues of designer-clad fashionistas waiting to enter Louis Vuitton's store in Omotesando, the largest in Tokyo.

Dominating the street with a 270-m- (886-ft-) façade, Omotesando Hills is a cutting-edge complex of fashion, art and entertainment. Reconstructed from the former Dojunkai Aoyama Apartments that were originally built in 1927, Omotesando Hills has successfully shed its retro image. Designed by Tadao Ando, one of Japan's most prominent architects, the glass frontage, angled extensions and roof gardens have become a bold and contemporary fashion statement. Housing close to 100 shops and restaurants, beauty spas and art galleries alongside 38 exclusive residential units, Omotesando Hills has become the focal point of Aoyama's shopping and residential area.

A stunning six-level atrium forms the heart of the main building, where the ground level is connected to the top floor by a 700-m- (2,297-ft-) tall spiral slope. Visitors to the mall will be enthralled by its electrifying atmosphere created by the ingenious merging of technology and creativity. A 250-m- (820-ft-) long LED 'bright-up wall' gives a luminous display of swirling colours and shapes, while wave speakers and a state-of-the-art sound system ensure exceptional clarity in the music, enhancing the already vibrant ambience. The overall effect is indeed startling as the dazzling colours and sophisticated architectural design create an interactive shopping environment in one of Tokyo's newest and most stylish fashion spots.

There are bags, shoes, jewellery, clothes, fashion accessories, home ware and stationery shops galore across the six vast floors of the mall. Visitors can find anything from an antique watch at Carese to doggy fashion—pets' clothing, collars and leashes—at Hannari. If pampering the pooch is not on the shopping agenda, then Porsche Design, Dolce & Gabbana, Jimmy Choo and Dunhill are just some of the world renowned brands found at the mall. With over 200 years of history and three Royal Warrants, Gieves & Hawkes brings the best in men's tailoring to Omotesando Hills, while Canadian based Arianne, which supplies camisoles, corsets among an exquisite range of lingerie for women, is another famous tenant. There is also a strong presence of Japanese designers here. Mitsuo Sato's

boutique, Bite Premium, sells beautifully handmade bags for men and women, while at De La Rose, Shu Uemura offers nearly every conceivable item that is related to flowers, including ladies' wear, fashion accessories, home products, make-up, food, books and music.

For the tired shopper, Le Boise Spa treats aching feet and shoulders with oriental herbal massages and reflexology treatments.

THIS PAGE (CLOCKWISE FROM TOP):
Tadao Ando's design gives the mall a modern and urban look; the beautiful roof garden adds to the vibrancy of the complex; with six levels of restaurants, shops and more, Omotesando Hills is a shopper's paradise.
OPPOSITE (FROM LEFT): *Sophistication and style are synonymous with Omotesando Hills; be it spring, summer, autumn or winter, Omotesando Hills will always attract the crowds.*

...an amazingly wide range of cuisines...

Hairdressers, beauty salons and cosmetic stores, including MAC, also cater to the sophisticated crowd the complex attracts.

First opened in 1974 in the old Dojunkai Aoyama Apartments and remaining on site in the redeveloped Omotesando Hills, Gallerie 412 is very much the link between the past and present. Over the years they have hosted exhibitions for famous artists such as Ben Shahn, Le Corbusier and Toko Shinoda. Replicating the décor of the former

apartments, another art gallery, Gallery Dojunkai, doubles up as an excellent spot to hold events in between exhibitions.

With an amazingly wide range of cuisines, as well as chocolates and sake, visitors will be spoilt for choice. Mist is an upmarket noodle shop while Yasaiya-Mei— serving fusion Japanese cuisine—offers healthy vegetable-based dishes and local grilled meat and fish delicacies. At Italian restaurants Trattoria and Pizzeria Zazza, the

aroma of Neapolitan home-style cooking will tempt shoppers' taste buds. For the more adventurous who want to taste something unique, Poivrier is the place to visit as it sells unusual spices, using ingredients such as seasonal freshly ground herbs for a healthy food and drinks menu. Bisty's is every wine lover's dream come true as guests can eat, drink and shop in this wine shop and brasserie with over 80 varieties of wine available for sampling.

FACTS

PRODUCTS	art galleries • dining • residences • shopping
FEATURES	Western and Japanese shops and restaurants • space 'o' • refurbished Dojunkai Aoyama Apartments
NEARBY	Harajuku Station • Meiji Shrine • Shibuya • Takeshita Street • Yoyogi Park
CONTACT	4-12-10 Jingumae, Shibuya-ku, Tokyo, 150-0001 • telephone: +81.3.3497 0310 • website: www.omotesandohills.com

PHOTOGRAPHS COURTESY OF MORI BUILDING CO. LTD.

Pleats Please Issey Miyake Aoyama

THIS PAGE (CLOCKWISE FROM TOP):
Combining vibrant and technological innovation, the pleats-themed designs will attract all fashionistas; the store in the heart of Aoyama's shopping district.

OPPOSITE (FROM LEFT): *Shoppers can find a wide variety of colours; Pleats Please Issey Miyake's bright and avant-garde décor exudes style and sophistication.*

Launched in 1993, Pleats Please Issey Miyake is one of the many clothing labels launched under the Issey Miyake umbrella. The simple shapes, diverse colours and avant-garde designs have created a dedicated following. The label operates independently today, and has freestanding boutiques in major cities like Paris, New York, London and not to mention Tokyo.

In Tokyo, Pleats Please Issey Miyake is housed near the Issey Miyake flagship store on La Place Minami Aoyama. Alongside

other renowned international labels, this quintessential Tokyo brand makes a strong presence in one of the most prestigious shopping districts in the city. Nearby, visitors can explore and experience the newly renovated and cutting-edge fashion complex of Omotesando Hills. To its west, Shibuya is characterised by giant TV screens, colourful neon lights and crowded streets. To its east is the dynamic Roppongi, the late night party district. Conveniently located within

...simple shapes, diverse colours and avant-garde designs...

techniques, such as processing and pleating material, and using them to create innovative products. In contrast to the standard pleating process, fabric is first cut and sewn before pleating. This allows the pleats to fall in a specific fashion, thus accentuating the contours of the body and creating a unique form to every garment.

The shop space is a striking, stark canvas with stone floor, bright windows and simple metal rails to complement the dynamism of the clothes' colours. In addition, Pleats Please Issey Miyake offers a huge variety of clothing. From fun, retro-style t-shirts in bright colours to versatile and sophisticated black pleated skirts, there is something for everyone. Oversized bows and other accessories are added as they enhance the characters in each design. Integrating the elements of elegance, sport and fun into their creations, Pleats Please Issey Miyake is universal, befitting every occasion and style.

At the new boutique in Roppongi, shoppers will discover an impressive range of merchandise. Apart from its trademark clothing, exclusive to this shop are Pleats Please Issey Miyake bags, accessories and even stationery. Incorporating the brand's philosophy, these products infuse practicality with avant-garde designs—imperative guidelines to touring Tokyo's most fashionable addresses.

walking distance of multiple subway stations, Aoyama is bustling with energy and has become the heart of Tokyo's fast evolving culture.

As its name implies, clothing at Pleats Please Issey Miyake features a multitude of pleats. Following Issey Miyake's fascination with technology in clothing design, the fundamental idea of Pleats Please Issey Miyake involves developing traditional

FACTS

PRODUCTS clothing • accessories

FEATURES spacious shop floor • avant-garde décor • dynamic and unique designs

NEARBY Aoyama • Harajuku • Meiji Shrine • Omotesando • Shibuya • Yoyogi Park

CONTACT La Place Minami Aoyama, 3-13-21 Minami-Aoyama, Minato-ku, Tokyo, 107-0062 • telephone: +81.3.5772 7750 • website: www.isseymiyake.com

PHOTOGRAPHS COURTESY OF ISSEY MIYAKE INC.

Roppongi Hills

Roppongi Hills, the largest private urban redevelopment in Japan to date, has redefined the cultural heart of Tokyo with more than 759,000 sq m (8,169,808 sq ft) dedicated to entertainment, shopping, dining and business. It is indeed a remarkable vision of 21st-century urban design that has taken over 17 years to cultivate. Now a sophisticated and lively hub for the arts, and with an observatory that offers a stunning city view, it is an inspiring location to begin a tour of Tokyo.

With offices interspersed with shops, restaurants, gardens, a gallery, museum, hotel, cinema, TV station and temple,

Roppongi Hills is aptly referred to as a 'city within a city'. Its streets bustle with activity, as office workers stream in and out of office buildings, tourists visit places of interest while locals go about their daily routine. In fact, city guides are on hand to help visitors experience the best of Roppongi Hills, which is certainly impressive. The tree-lined pedestrian walkways are beautifully manicured with surrounding flowerbeds and water features. Specially commissioned public works of art and design are also exhibited across the enormous site, enlivening the open spaces and creating bold contrasts to the blossoming trees.

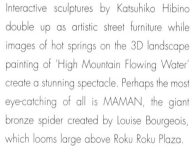

Interactive sculptures by Katsuhiko Hibino double up as artistic street furniture while images of hot springs on the 3D landscape painting of 'High Mountain Flowing Water' create a stunning spectacle. Perhaps the most eye-catching of all is MAMAN, the giant bronze spider created by Louise Bourgeois, which looms large above Roku Roku Plaza.

Rising high above the rest, Mori Tower is the soaring symbol of Roppongi Hills. With 54 floors, it is instantly recognised across the cityscape as one of the tallest buildings in Japan. Although it houses mostly state-of-the-art financial and IT firms, the top floors are dedicated to public use with the Tokyo City View observatory and the Mori Art Museum.

...a remarkable vision of 21st-century urban design that has taken over 17 years to cultivate.

Take a ride up to the 52nd floor, where the observatory offers breathtaking 360-degree views of the city. The central location that Roppongi Hills enjoys becomes immediately apparent as the visitor takes in the magnificent sights of the nearby skyscrapers of Shinjuku, the grand Imperial Palace and Tokyo Tower. In addition, unique shops and cafés add to the vibrancy of the place. At an amazing 250 m (820 ft) above sea level, shopping and dining take on a whole new experience altogether. For nature lovers, the waters of Tokyo Bay and the majestic Mount Fuji—resembling the city's guardian angel—lie just over the horizon.

Located on the 53rd floor, the Mori Art Museum promotes a diverse range of contemporary art from its stunning gallery

in the sky. Enjoying strong rapport with its counterparts around the world, exhibitions held at the museum cover an array of fields that includes fashion, architecture, design and photography. In addition, there is Academyhills, an excellent forum for intellectual exchanges with its state-of-the-art facilities, including a sophisticated library. Along with Roppongi Hills Club, these facilities make up the Mori Arts Center, symbolising Roppongi Hills' position as the 'cultural heart of Tokyo'.

THIS PAGE (FROM TOP): the Conran-designed residences exude style and sophistication; one of the intriguing public arts on display, titled 'Annas Stenar' by Thomas Sandell, 2003.

OPPOSITE (FROM LEFT): Karim Rashid's sKape, 2003, captures the public's attention; cherry blossom trees encapsulate the beauty of Roppongi Hills.

There is an outdoor arena that stages live performances and celebrations. In the early mornings during summertime, residents can be seen practising tai chi here. Live bands perform both traditional and modern music and collaborate with dancers in various gigs. During any celebratory occasion, the area will come alive and be abuzz with entertainment and festivities.

A replica of a 17th-century Japanese garden and cocooned by the futuristic towers of Roppongi Hills, the Mohri Garden provides the perfect refuge from the frenetic world outside. With lush greenery and a beautiful waterfall, the garden acts like an urban sanctuary, its peace and quiet providing a welcome change from the frantic atmosphere of surrounding streets.

An excellent alternative to the famed shopping districts of Omotesando and Ginza, Roppongi Hills is host to over 230 restaurants and shops boasting everything from luxury Western brands to stylish Asian designer names. Spread across boutique-style lanes and huge shopping malls, Roppongi Hills features the best of the UK at Harrods and some of the world's most stunning jewellery at Tiffany & Co., not to mention the ever popular Birkenstock, beautifully designed handbags from Kate

THIS PAGE (FROM TOP): Shops and food galore at Roppongi Hills; apart from the museum and art gallery, visitors can soak up the bustling shopping atmosphere.

OPPOSITE: The amazing giant bronze spider, MAMAN, is a remarkable sight.

Spade and dazzling evening wear by Hong Kong designer Vivienne Tam. Appealing to all markets, Banana Republic, Zara, Maxmara and Armani can be found too.

Running through the heart of Roppongi Hills, Keyakizaka Street is lined with beautiful zelkova trees. On either side, the world's most luxurious brands, including Hugo Boss and Louis Vuitton, are advertised through creative window displays and visitors come as much for the spectacle as they do for the shopping. Running alongside the 400-m- (1,312-ft-) Keyakizaka Street, street furniture is erected between the trees, combining nature and art with the thrill of shopping.

Three shopping malls—West Walk, Hill Side and Metro Hat—are home to the majority of shops at Roppongi Hills. Strikingly different, each mall possesses a unique style and design. With sharp edges, angled bridges and glass flooring, West Walk features a five-level galleria creating a metal ravine down to the bustling ground floor. The atrium is lined with international fashion boutiques including Zara and Johanna Ho and restaurants from around the world. In bold contrast, with soft and sloping features, Hill Side remains semi-open with outdoor walkways above a traditional Japanese garden. Its four floors are home to exquisite interior design shops such as Living and Musée Imaginaire, and an impressive

collection of local and Asian designers, featuring Anna Sui and Keita Maruyama. An Asian prominence can also be felt in the multitude of Asian restaurants and traditional teahouses. Metro Hat makes up the main entrance to Roppongi Hills, directly connected to the subway at Roppongi Station, and complete with delicious take-out delicatessens.

Just as celebrated for its wonderfully diverse range of cuisines, almost any flavour and cooking style, from rustic French to gourmet Japanese, can be found at Roppongi Hills. Cafés, restaurants and bars offer a wide spectrum of choices, be it an al fresco lunch for two or a glamorous evening of cocktails and champagne. The exclusive Roppongi Hills Club, designed by Sir Terence Conran, incorporates seven

restaurants and a bar that cater to a stylish crowd. From the 51st floor of the Mori Tower, spectacular views can be admired from just about every corner. At Fifty-One, the Club's signature restaurant, smart black leather chairs, chrome pillars and a panorama of the startling skyscrapers below

THIS PAGE (FROM TOP): The City and Land section of the 'Africa Remix: Contemporary Art of a Continent' exhibition at the Mori Art Museum, 2006; visitors will be thrilled to discover a variety of cuisines that cater to every palate.

OPPOSITE (FROM LEFT): Night or day, the breathtaking city skyline at the Tokyo City View observatory is mesmerising; the museum is given a stylish décor, as befits a place with equally avant-garde exhibits.

...any flavour and cooking style, from rustic French to gourmet Japanese, can be found...

While Grand Hyatt Tokyo and the Conran-designed residences do provide upmarket and luxurious accommodation in the area for those seeking to pamper themselves, Roppongi Hills remains largely an exciting centre for all to visit, absorb and enjoy some of Tokyo's most attractive sights, shopping and dining experiences.

create a spectacular setting. With plenty of dining options, guests will be spoilt for choice as they can enjoy Japanese cuisine from Hyakumi-an's slate bar or go French at The French Cellar, which possesses one of the most impressive wine cellars in the city. The cosy Sushi Bar seats an intimate nine people for an elite dinner while Italian restaurant, La Cucina, and its Chinese counterpart, Star Anise, offer family-style lunches and dinners. After a satisfying meal, take in the magnificent view of Tokyo's skyline and indulge in a Cosmopolitan at the same time at Club's sophisticated bar.

FACTS

PRODUCTS	cinema • city tours • dining • gardens • museum • offices • shopping
FEATURES	Academyhills • Conran-designed residences • Grand Hyatt Tokyo • Mori Art Museum • the Mohri Garden • Roppongi Hills Club • Tokyo City View
NEARBY	Akasaka • Azabu-Juban • Roppongi • Shibuya
CONTACT	Direct link by concourse to Roppongi Station • Mori Art Museum: +81.3.5777 8600 • Tokyo City View: +81.3.6406 6652 • Roppongi Hills Tours: +81.3.6406 6677 • website: www.roppongihills.com

NAGOMI Spa + Fitness

THIS PAGE: Take a swim, or relax by the unique red granite pool.

OPPOSITE (CLOCKWISE FROM LEFT): Soft lighting in the NAGOMI suite ensures a relaxing ambience; look forward to an indulging spa experience in the well-equipped treatment room; the Japanese stone bath in its sleek setting.

Located on the fifth floor of Grand Hyatt Tokyo, NAGOMI Spa and Fitness, with its sophisticated and stylish décor, is a prestigious addition to the fashionable, designer-led development of Roppongi Hills.

Nagomi means harmony, well-being, balance and relaxation, and the spa certainly offers revitalising treatments that refresh both mind and body. Harnessing the natural goodness found in water, mud, salts, essential oils and thermal stones, NAGOMI combines traditional and innovative methods in its treatments for men and women.

The spa's signature massage begins with a relaxing foot bath and exfoliation. A full body massage, using a personalised blend

...offers revitalising treatments that refresh both mind and body.

Sixty minutes of an invigorating exfoliation using thermal salt rich in minerals is further boosted by a camomile loofah scrub that leaves one feeling pleasantly refreshed.

Following the ancient tradition of the Spa Kurs that uses natural ingredients, NAGOMI offers its own Herbal, Thermal or Thalasso Kur, which is tailored to suit personal needs. In three stages over 2 hours, the guest is treated to a scrub or wrap, a stimulating bath and a luxurious massage.

A remarkable relaxation area of sandstone and wood is dominated by the equally magnificent red granite swimming pool. Treatment suites, which also cater for couples, possess their own Japanese stone bath, steam shower and bathroom. Other facilities include a whirlpool, plunge pools, saunas and an advanced fitness room.

Having restored the inner-self, the spa offers a wide range of manicures, pedicures and paraffin wax treatments for the complete NAGOMI experience.

of oils, follows. The healing elements of water form an integral aspect of the NAGOMI treatment. Body scrubs are combined with Vichy hydrotherapy to enhance the overall soothing experience. Starting with a rain shower, the Turkish Salt Scrub is followed by a two-step treatment.

FACTS

PRODUCTS	facials • massages • spa kurs • manicures and pedicures • spa cuisine
FEATURES	fitness centre • whirlpool • personal training • plunge pools • pool • sauna
NEARBY	Roppongi Hills • Roppongi Subway Station • Ginza • Kasumigaseki District
CONTACT	5F Grand Hyatt Tokyo, 6-10-3 Roppongi, Minato-ku, Tokyo, 106-0032 • telephone: +81.3.4333 1234 • facsimile: +81.3.4333 8123 • email: info@tyogh.com • website: www.tokyo.grand.hyatt.com

PHOTOGRAPHS COURTESY OF GRAND HYATT TOKYO.

YU, The Spa

The hot spring, with water brought in from Ito on the Izu Peninsula, is one of the many exceptional facilities. There are also Japanese cedar baths, dry saunas, a fitness gym and hydraulic Vichy showers.

Spa suites contain an indoor treatment area with a traditional Japanese garden and an outdoor bath set in a dynamic environment of rich natural colours, soft lighting and delicate Japanese furnishings. The VIP suite, 115 sq m (1,238 sq ft) in size, encompasses large indoor and outdoor daybeds and an open-air onsen bath and shower. With packages tailored for couples complete with personalised services, YU, The Spa offers a blissful hideaway that ranks among the city's most exclusive experiences.

Treatments at YU use the signature Four Seasons oils that are created from seasonal herbs and flowers found in the Chinzan-so

THIS PAGE (FROM TOP): YU's indoor heated pool makes swimming possible all year round; the poolside lounge is an excellent place to relax, before or after a swim.

OPPOSITE (CLOCKWISE FROM LEFT): With both indoor and outdoor daybeds, the spacious VIP room offers a most indulgent experience; the Vichy rain shower will leave guests thoroughly refreshed; the avant-garde lobby entrance of YU.

A magnificent swimming pool with a retractable roof; an outdoor jacuzzi complete with its own waterfall. Indeed, sophistication hangs in the air of YU, The Spa at Four Seasons Hotel Tokyo at Chinzan-so. In its tranquil setting, guests can expect a relaxing and indulgent experience as they savour the nutritious delights of spa cuisine and unwind at the spa's impressive facilities, including a personalised poolside service.

...offers a blissful hideaway that ranks among the city's most exclusive experiences.

Gardens. Blending both Japanese and Western influences, ingredients include wasabi and sake tonic with extracts from ginger, carrot, coriander and juniper.

A Fire and Water Purification treatment is also available. As with the Shugendo tradition of the 12th century, in which Buddhist monks sought to achieve the perfect state of being by undergoing a series of purification rites, this treatment strives to achieve the same result. It starts with a sage and cypress body wash followed by a sake and salt polish before it is rinsed away with a warm Vichy rain shower. The Fire therapy then begins on a pre-warmed massage bed for a body massage that strengthens the pressure points, ending with a five-grain body wrap and an eye compress with refreshing basil gel.

Extravagance, an indulgent facial treatment, is exactly what the name suggests. A rose cleanser and intensive skin serum are used for the face. For a back massage, pure rose body oil is used. After a frankincense oil scalp massage, the session is rounded off with a moisturising pure rose mask.

FACTS

PRODUCT	body treatments • facial treatments • hand and foot treatments • massages • salon services
FEATURES	fitness gym • Guerlain Salon • hot spring • jacuzzi • pool • sauna • spa boutique • spa lounge
NEARBY	Chinzan-so Gardens • Ikebukuro • Mejiro Station
CONTACT	Four Seasons Hotel Tokyo at Chinzan-so, 2-10-8 Sekiguchi, Bunkyo-ku, Tokyo, 112-8667 • telephone: +81.3.3943 6958 • facsimile: +81.3.3943 1255 • email: tokyo.concierge@fourseasons.com • website: www.fourseasons.com/tokyo

PHOTOGRAPHS COURTESY OF FOUR SEASONS HOTEL TOKYO AT CHINZAN-SO.

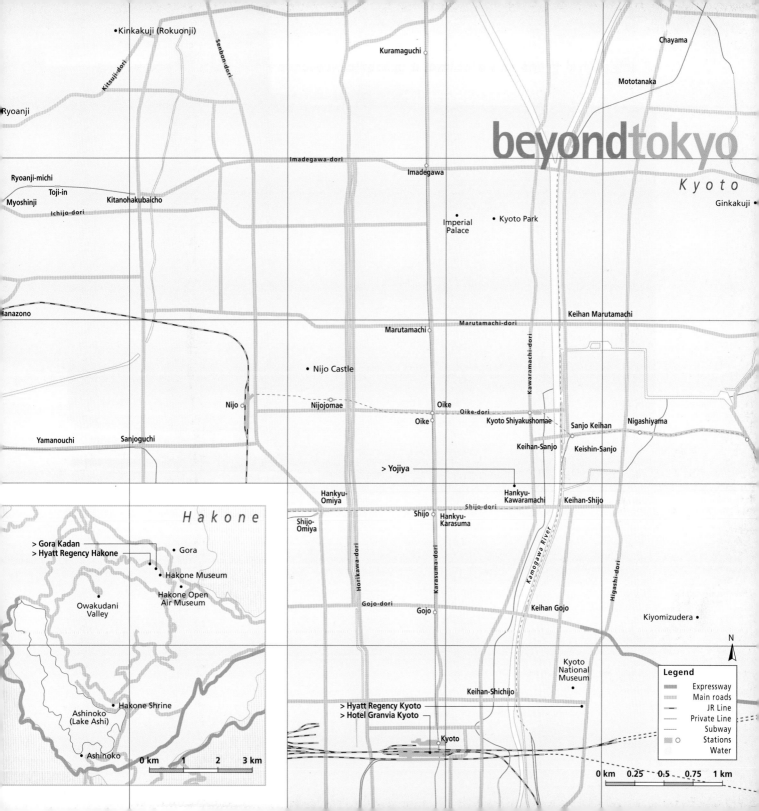

beyondtokyo
Kyoto

- Kinkakuji (Rokuonji)
- Kuramaguchi
- Chayama
- Mototanaka
- Ryoanji
- Kitsuji-dori
- Senbon-dori
- Imadegawa-dori
- Imadegawa
- Ginkakuji
- Ryoanji-michi
- Toji-in
- Myoshinji
- Kitanohakubaicho
- Ichijo-dori
- Imperial Palace
- Kyoto Park
- Hanazono
- Keihan Marutamachi
- Marutamachi-dori
- Marutamachi
- Nijo Castle
- Kawaramachi-dori
- Nijo
- Nijojomae
- Oike
- Oike-dori
- Oike
- Kyoto Shiyakushomae
- Sanjo Keihan
- Nigashiyama
- Yamanouchi
- Sanjoguchi
- Keihan-Sanjo
- Keishin-Sanjo
- > Yojiya
- Hankyu-Omiya
- Hankyu-Kawaramachi
- Keihan-Shijo
- Shijo-Omiya
- Shijo-dori
- Shijo
- Hankyu-Karasuma
- Horikawa-dori
- Karasuma-dori
- Kamogawa River
- Higashi-dori
- Gojo-dori
- Gojo
- Keihan Gojo
- Kiyomizudera
- Kyoto National Museum
- Keihan-Shichijo
- > Hyatt Regency Kyoto
- > Hotel Granvia Kyoto
- Kyoto

Hakone

- > Gora Kadan
- > Hyatt Regency Hakone
- Gora
- Hakone Museum
- Hakone Open Air Museum
- Owakudani Valley
- Hakone Shrine
- Ashinoko (Lake Ashi)
- Ashinoko

| 0 km | 1 | 2 | 3 km |

N

Legend

	Expressway
	Main roads
	JR Line
	Private Line
	Subway
○	Stations
	Water

| 0 km | 0.25 | 0.5 | 0.75 | 1 km |

away from it all

Tokyo may be one of the world's biggest and most exciting cities, but it is far from all that Japan has to offer. When Tokyoites want to recharge their batteries or just enjoy a change of scenery, there is no shortage of other places they can go.

One popular day-trip destination is Kamakura, just under an hour south of Tokyo by train. Situated in a leafy valley near several beaches outside the mouth of Tokyo Bay, Kamakura is a small, quiet getaway with a spectacular past. This sleepy little town, popular with Tokyo-dwelling surfers thanks to its gentle but rideable waves, was actually the nation's capital during the eponymous Kamakura period (1192–1333), and the shoguns who ruled from this place left as their legacy an abundance of Buddhist temples and Shinto shrines. One of the best-known sights in all of Japan, in fact, is the Great Buddha at Kamakura's Kotoku-in temple. This 93-tonne, 13.5-m-(44-ft-) high seated figure usually looks quite serene against its backdrop of trees and sky, but it was originally intended to be sheltered inside a cavernous wooden hall. However, a not-so-gentle wave, of the tsunami variety, struck the city in 1495, sweeping the wooden building away and leaving the Buddha exposed to the sky, with which it has communed ever since.

Tokyoites who prefer mountainous scenery take off in the opposite direction, north, to the small city of Nikko. It's one of the most popular spots in Japan to watch the leaves change colour in the autumn, but its chief year-round attraction is Toshogu Shrine, the burial place of the shogun Ieyasu Tokugawa. The shrine's elaborately carved and colourfully painted eaves include a variety of intriguing figures, most notably a trio of monkeys in the classic 'see no evil, hear no evil, speak no evil' pose that, according to legend, originated here as a subtle comment on the harshness of the shoguns' rule. Despite attracting visitors from Tokyo for nearly 400 years, Nikko remains a place of great natural beauty, noted for the 163-m- (535-ft) deep Chuzenjiko (Lake Chuzenji), the 97-m (318-ft) cataract of Kegon Falls, and numerous rejuvenating onsen hot springs.

PAGE 168: A woman in a smart kimono makes her way down a grand staircase in Kyoto.

THIS PAGE: Forever serene, the Great Buddha of Kamakura lets the centuries roll off his shoulders as easily as the rain.

OPPOSITE: Kegon Falls tumbles out of Chuzenjiko in Nikko, in the mountains north of Tokyo.

Yokohama, Japan's second-largest city, acted as Tokyo's gateway to the world before the age of aviation. As Japan's first internationalised city, it still has the nation's largest Chinatown. Yokohama was heavily developed in the Meiji period, and a large number of stone or brick buildings from that era are still in use, including several made into a trendy shopping mall—suitably called Yokohama Red Brick Warehouse. But Yokohama also looks towards the future and is the site of Japan's tallest building, the handsomely tapered, 70-storey Yokohama Landmark Tower.

Visiting Kamakura is like making a trip back to the 13th century, while Nikko represents the 17th century, and Yokohama combines elements of the 19th to the 21st. In contrast to all of these, Hakone, nestled at the foot of Mount Fuji, is simply timeless.

the allure of fuji-san

Geological formations are almost never described as chic, but an exception must be made in the case of Mount Fuji. Always above it all, yet somehow never aloof, Fuji-san subtly adjusts her classic good looks to fit the season or the time of day. Japanese artists of every medium have employed her as model and muse for centuries, but still she has

preserved her mystique by avoiding overexposure. Spending much of her time veiled in mist or swathed in clouds, Fuji-san guarantees that her unexpected appearances are momentous occasions when people from miles around stop what they are doing and pay her the attention that her beauty demands. The suffix '-san', by the way, literally means mountain, but in this mountain's case it is a meaningful coincidence that the same syllable (written differently) is also used as a human title of respect.

For aesthetically inclined Tokyoites, simply admiring Fuji-san from afar is not always enough. The resort area of Hakone is a favourite place to get a little closer without having to lace up a pair of hiking boots. But for the more active types, the mountain is open in July and August when more than 180,000 adventurous climbers attempt the hours-long, lung-shredding ascent to the 3,776-m- (12,388-ft-) summit. For all her loveliness, Fuji-san sometimes punishes those who get too close.

However, Hakone, nestled comfortably in the far more accessible, forest-covered mountains that stand between Fuji-san's lofty snow-capped peak and the deep blue waters of Sagami Bay, is a place where tranquillity and relaxation are the order of the day. Except, perhaps, for the first few days of each year.

ABOVE: Gnarled pines and graceful Mount Fuji are popular motifs in Japanese art.

THIS PAGE: Jingle bells left behind by Mount Fuji visitors who had attached them to walking sticks for their nighttime climb.

OPPOSITE: A modern umbrella and a traditional one work equally well for these two Shinto priests climbing steps in Kamakura.

hakone ekiden: running to and fro

Lots of people want to go from Tokyo to Hakone, but it takes a special kind of person—or group of people—to literally run there. Specifically, it takes the track teams of 20 major Japanese universities, competing against each other in the Hakone Ekiden, an annual relay race with a history dating back more than 80 years. Starting and finishing in front of the headquarters of the main sponsor, *The Yomiuri Shimbun* newspaper, the young athletes transport a symbolic sash all the way to Hakone and back, about 218 km (135½ miles) in total. Exhausted runners hand the sash to their team-mates at transition points spaced roughly every 21 km (13 miles). The race from Tokyo takes place on January 2, with the return trip made the next day.

Illustrating the prized Japanese values of persistence, endurance and teamwork, the nationally televised race draws a wide audience, with alumni from the participating schools tuning in with high hopes that their alma mater will be the first to get its team across the finish line.

The Hakone turnaround point is the eastern shore of Ashinoko (Lake Ashi). Televised glimpses of the scenery here, and of the tree-lined roads that lead in and out, serve to remind those watching at home what a gorgeous area Hakone is. Presumably, this prompts more than a few viewers to pencil in possible trips here on their brand-new calendars.

Ashinoko is a relatively narrow lake, but it is nearly 20 km (12½ miles) long. The western end of the lake points almost directly at Fuji-san, providing memorable views from the east—that is, when she chooses to reveal herself. Whether or not Fuji-san appears, the wooded slopes immediately surrounding the lake are beautiful in their own right. The trees on the north shore give seclusion to the Hakone Shrine, whose location is nonetheless clearly marked by a magnificent red torii

standing out in the water, very much in the style of the national icon torii that stands in the sea at Miyajima, near Hiroshima. The eastern end of the lake and a few other spots in the area sometimes feel a bit touristy, with swan boats for rent and a full-size replica of a Disney-esque pirate ship plying the waters. However, a short drive into the woods is all it takes to leave the masses behind and transport yourself straight back to the peace and quiet.

resting in the forest

The lush greenery of the Hakone area is enough to make you forget that downtown Tokyo is a mere 2 hours away. Wild boars still roam in these forests of cedar and

beech, where the underbrush appears thick and healthy even in the more shady areas. Sasa, a slender but very leafy variety of bamboo, grows in thick profusion above the moss-softened stone or concrete embankments of the narrow roads, while tall, feathery pampas grass characterises the forests' sunny clearings.

The roads in the Hakone area, especially in the town of Gora, snake back on themselves over and over as they wind their way up the mountain slopes; they are so steep in places that the headlights of cars making the ascent at night seem like searchlights sweeping skyward. Gora, sheltered behind a row of mountains from the lake, is also the terminus of the quaint Hakone Tozan Train, a toy-like conveyance that zigzags higher and higher on a single track, picking its way through tunnels and along trestles over gorges until at last it can go no further, and passengers wishing to continue over the top of the mountains must transfer to a funicular railway that tackles the slopes head on.

The topography here is as wrinkled and folded in on itself as the convolutions of the human brain. And much like the brain, Gora has its secrets, particularly in the form of chic little hideaways nestled in the rocks and trees, exemplified by the ryokan (a traditional Japanese inn), Gora Kadan. Its private dining rooms ensure that moans of

THIS PAGE (FROM TOP): Japanese maple trees, with leaves like tiny, waving hands, give this garden a classical feel; yukata bathrobes await guests at a ryokan, with their cloth belts folded neatly on top; wooden sandals for a stroll around the garden.
OPPOSITE: The red torii of Hakone Shrine stands in the serene waters of Ashinoko.

pleasure will not be overheard as guests sample the multiple courses of its meticulously prepared kaiseki cuisine, and its spa shows what can be done with the area's abundant and healing hot spring water.

This mineral-rich water, a gift from the warm, volcanic heart of Mount Fuji, bubbles up from underground at various points in the Hakone area. The alkaline water here is said to be good for your skin, and one leisurely dip is enough to prove it. Yet, as desirable as a silky epidermis may be, an even greater benefit of a hot spring soak is its soothing effect on the psyche. There are few experiences more relaxing. At the Hyatt Regency Hakone Resort and Spa, the flowing waters are enhanced with locally produced herbal products. Under the right circumstances, tension and worry are seemingly water-soluble.

For those who would rather sightsee than soak, the funicular railway—a tram on rails so steep that it must be pulled along by a cable—over the nearest peak will take them toward Owakudani, an unearthly landscape of bare rocks and sulphurous steam. The Hakone area is known for its many onsen hot springs, in which volcanically heated, mineral-rich water seeps or bubbles to the surface in pleasantly usable quantities. At Owakudani, however, the loudly gurgling water flows in such abundance that it overwhelms the landscape. In the early evening darkness, when gigantic wisps of steam writhe across the face of the rising moon like dragon's breath, Owakudani can resemble the set of an old-time horror film—albeit a beautifully filmed one.

the hakone open-air museum

Hakone is well known for its man-made beauty as well as the natural kind, and one of its top attractions is a place that combines both. The superb Hakone Open-Air Museum is the best known of the area's numerous art museums and galleries, and with good reason too.

The first thing one sees upon entering this museum is Carl Milles' 1949 sculpture *Man and Pegasus*. It's impossible to miss, mounted on a towering 9-m- (29½-ft-) pedestal that lifts it into silhouette against the sky above a nearby valley, making it appear that the winged horse and his rider are truly in flight. Meanwhile, on the ground, Antoine Bourdelle's 1909 sculpture *Hercules the Archer* appears to be aiming his bow at the flying pair, while Auguste Rodin's portly 1890s *Balzac*, robed like a judge, looks on in seeming disapproval.

Don't let the humorous interplay of these three works give the impression that the Open-Air Museum doesn't take art seriously. With grounds that undulate across 7 hectares (17 acres) of mountainside, each item in its large collection—which includes sculptures

by Taro Okamoto, Henry Moore, Niki de Saint Phalle and Alexander Calder—is given plenty of room to breathe. Each piece can be appreciated on its own, despite the whimsical juxtapositions that become apparent from certain angles. There are also several small indoor galleries on the museum grounds, including one devoted exclusively to Pablo Picasso that focuses mainly on his ceramic works.

Despite a look-but-don't-touch policy for most of the collection, the spirit of the Open-Air Museum is clearly interactive with visitors cheerfully striking imitative poses in front of statues while friends snap pictures. In a few special cases, such as a 3D crystal maze or an upside-down 'castle' of nets hanging from the roof of an open-sided pavilion, children are actually encouraged to climb on the art.

Seeing everything here takes quite a bit of walking. Those who wish to rest their feet are invited to do so in the museum's public outdoor footbath, a long, curving trough supplied with a continuous stream of local hot spring water.

THIS PAGE: Sculptures at the spacious Hakone Open-Air Museum can always be enjoyed in natural light.

OPPOSITE (FROM LEFT): A family of bathers enjoys a gravity-powered back massage; hot spring water flows into a private tub at the Hyatt Regency Hakone Resort and Spa.

the pola museum of art

If the Open-Air Museum is exuberant, then the Pola Museum of Art is discreet. Built on the principle of a coexistence between nature and art, the three-storey museum, which opened in 2002, is sunk deep into a hillside to ensure it has a minimal impact on the surrounding landscape. Indeed, it is almost invisible until you are upon it. Despite being semi-subterranean, the museum's central atrium does get plenty of sunlight, while the galleries off to either side are artificially lit using up-to-the-minute fibre optic technology which helps preserve the exhibited works they house.

The Pola displays paintings by various artists including Manet, Monet, Renoir, Seurat, Pissarro, Gauguin, Cézanne, Dalí, Magritte, Chagall, Picasso, Kandinsky, Miró—a virtual who's who of mid-19th-to-mid-20th-century Western art. But there is plenty of Japanese art, too, demonstrating what happened on the Eastern side of the world during more than a century of East-West artistic interplay. Even as Japonisme was taking off in Europe, Japanese artists were learning Western painting techniques and using them to portray traditional Japanese themes. Good examples here include Okada Saburosuke's 1927 oil painting of a Japanese woman draped in a kimono and Koyama Shotaro's 1890 scene of travelling samurai stopping at a rural inn for a drink.

The museum had its genesis in the private collection of the late Tsuneshi Suzuki, owner of the Pola Group, a Japanese cosmetics giant. Suzuki collected a staggering 9,500 works over a 40-year period and considering the source of Suzuki's

wealth, it is no surprise that the museum also features items of beauty. The collection includes Edo period (1603–1867) Japanese hair ornaments; an array of handcrafted combs from around the world in mother-of-pearl, lacquer, tortoiseshell and wood; perfume bottles by Emile Gallé; and a bridal cosmetic set in lacquer. Self-guided tours of the museum are available, using an English-language headphone service.

lalique museum

The newest of Hakone's major art showcases is the Lalique Museum Hakone, which opened in 2005. French jeweller and glassmaker René Lalique (1860–1945) often used birds, flowers, insects and the female form as decorative motifs in his works; elements that might recall traditional Japanese aesthetic sensibilities. One of the larger items on display here is a gleaming 1928 Bugatti Type 57, which is equipped with a Lalique hood ornament—a Jurassic-sized dragonfly with wings of glass.

The museum displays about 230 pieces from its 1,500-item collection at any one time and the pieces span from Art Nouveau to Art Deco in style. There are many examples of the chic perfume bottles that made Lalique's name, as well as jewellery, vases, mirrors and a chalice modelled on a pinecone. Larger items include furniture, mantelpieces and a 1902 mould for the door to his Paris atelier. The door is crossed by friezes of nude youths in ambiguous poses—are they engaged in combat or play?—that call to mind the chaotic groupings of bodies in Rodin's earlier work, *The Gates of Hell*, on display back in Tokyo, in Ueno Park. By far the biggest exhibit at the Lalique Museum is the restored Orient Express railway carriage, where visitors can sit down and admire the Lalique-designed interior while sipping tea.

The appeal of Art Nouveau in Japan is not limited to Lalique. His contemporary, the artist Alphonse Mucha, is so popular that his colour drawings of women with dramatically flowing hair appear on the labels of Japanese coffee cans.

THIS PAGE (FROM TOP): The Pola Museum of Art, built to have a minimal impact on the forest; three swallows adorn a perfume bottle at the Lalique Museum; a vintage Bugatti with a glass dragonfly hood ornament.

OPPOSITE: The atrium of the Pola Museum makes full use of the existing natural light.

the old tokaido road

Long before its museums were built or the ekiden relay was run, Hakone was best known as the location of a checkpoint on the old Tokaido road. It was one of the outermost defences of Japan's capital during the Edo period. When the Tokugawa shoguns controlled Japan from Edo, their main lifeline to the rest of the nation was the Tokaido road, an ancient highway winding its way towards the former capital of Kyoto, some 370 km (230 miles) to the west. There were many checkpoints along this road (some of them in Edo itself) but Hakone's location, pinched between Mount Fuji and Sagami Bay, with Ashinoko as an additional barrier, made it a natural choke point.

Merchants, pilgrims, and other travellers could be examined here on their way in and out of the capital area, and even daimyo feudal lords living under the shogun's policy of alternate residence would pass through on a regular basis, accompanied by large retinues of samurai and servants. Offering a taste of those bygone days, portions of the old, stone-paved road have been preserved near the east end of the lake. These

THIS PAGE: On an ancient route, a Shinkansen bullet train passes Fuji-san on its way to Kyoto.

OPPOSITE (FROM TOP): Traditional Japan abounds in Kyoto; the gardens at Saiho-ji temple, also known as Koke-dera, are said to include 120 different varieties of moss.

segments of the old Tokaido road may be good for a scenic stroll, but anyone who really wants to travel between Tokyo and Kyoto nowadays can just hop on a Shinkansen bullet train. Fittingly, this modern rail route is named after the old highway. It's the Tokaido Shinkansen.

green kyoto

Tokyo and Kyoto are as alike—and as different—as two sisters. Tokyo is the younger, louder and flashier of the two. People outside the family tend to notice her first, yet they soon become enchanted with her quiet, reserved and graceful older sister, Kyoto.

Seen from afar, Tokyo is a tall and glittering megalopolis, while Kyoto is a low-rise, deceptively modest-looking city spreading out just enough to comfortably fill the valley floor on which it rests. Both cities are endlessly photogenic—but for different reasons. Tokyo is ultra-modern, while Kyoto is where old Japan most clearly survives, with rain-blackened wooden structures everywhere and abundant vegetation softening the scene. Hedges, vines and old-fashioned tile roofs abound.

Also in abundance are the trees—an estimated 50,000 of them in Kyoto Gyoen National Garden alone. This park in the centre of town was once a city within a city, containing the vast, walled grounds of the emperor's palace, with 200 aristocratic homes arrayed in close orbit around it. The complex fell into disrepair after the imperial court moved to Tokyo, but the old palace and a few other buildings were eventually preserved. The rest were cleared away to make room for the greenery.

Ten blocks away stands Nijo Castle, from which the Tokugawa shogun's deputies kept a watchful eye on the palace during the Edo period. The grounds provide another massive oasis of greenery, while the landscaped precincts of Kyoto's innumerable temples and shrines add even more to the foliage.

In addition to the green public spaces are the secret gardens of the machiya (townhouses). During the long peace of the Edo period, merchants in Kyoto built up significant wealth but were discouraged from flaunting it. They were legally prohibited from owning homes more than one storey tall, and their buildings were taxed according to the width of their frontage. Merchants responded by developing the machiya style of architecture: a house-cum-workplace with a tiny façade fronting a long, narrow interior extending far back from the street. Nicknamed 'eels' beds' for their unusual proportions, machiya included petite courtyards to provide air and sunlight. These courtyards became the sites of tiny but exquisitely crafted gardens that can still be enjoyed by visitors to the shops, restaurants and inns that some machiya have nowadays become.

Machiya symbolise a significant feature of Kyoto aesthetics: discreet grandeur. Beauty is everywhere, but it doesn't advertise itself very loudly. You have to slow down and look closely to appreciate Kyoto's charms, in contrast to the hustle of on-the-go Tokyo.

mountains set the scene

As in Tokyo, much of Kyoto's urban life is organised around a river that runs from north to south along the east side of town. But unlike Tokyo's Sumida River, a commercial artery easily navigable by large boats, Kyoto's Kamo River looks almost decorative. This shallow waterway meanders languidly among grassy islets, with stately white herons promenading through the ripples in search of minnows. Its high, well-maintained banks are famous as a romantic spot for Kyoto couples to stroll arm-in-arm, share a kiss, or just sit and watch the world go by.

The Kamo is one of several small rivers flowing down from the low, green mountains that surround the ancient capital. Because Kyoto has so few tall buildings, it is these mountains, some of them humped like the coils of a storybook sea serpent, that give the city's skyline its character. In August, gigantic fires are lit in the shape of pictures and kanji writing on five mountains to the north and west of the city in honour of the Bon season. So large, the fires can be seen from anywhere in the city.

Deep into the mountains of the north, there is a restaurant retreat called Miyamasou, or 'beautiful mountain lodge'. Here, amid forested surroundings, the cuisine of chef Hisato Nakahigashi highlights fish, fruit and vegetables produced in the region. On a mountain to the southeast, on the edge of the city, you will find the Fushimi Inari Shrine, whose long pathways, lined with hundreds of red torii (temple gates), were the setting for one of the few scenes in the movie *Memoirs of a Geisha* that were actually filmed in Kyoto. (Most of it was shot in California.)

A taste of history is available about 2 km (1¼ miles) south of the shrine, in an old machiya, which houses Chef Shigeo Araki's Uosaburou restaurant, founded in 1764.

THIS PAGE: The Fushimi Inari Shrine is known for its paths lined with long rows of torii. OPPOSITE (FROM TOP): A torii is depicted in lines of fire on a mountainside above the city; two women enjoy a sunny lunch on a footbridge over a tributary of the Kamo River.

The door of this establishment is remarkably still scarred by large bullet holes that were made during the days of turmoil that accompanied the 19th-century regime change from the rule of the last shogun to that of Emperor Meiji. Referring to Hollywood again, this was the period of fighting depicted in the film *The Last Samurai*.

The soft backdrop of mountains has an effect on how well—or how badly—modern architectural additions fit into the city. For instance, the space-age concrete pylon that is Kyoto Tower may have looked pretty groovy when it first went up in 1964, but the 131-m- (430-ft-) structure, much like the word 'groovy', has not aged well. It aggressively calls attention to itself in a city where discretion is the rule.

Starchitect Tadao Ando understood that rule when he designed the Garden of Fine Arts in northern Kyoto in 1994. An outdoor gallery of high-tech reproductions, painted masterpieces are displayed on ceramic plates that are completely weatherproof. Ando placed the bulk of the 'stroll garden' below ground level so as not to interfere with existing views of the mountains from the adjacent Kyoto Botanical Gardens.

On a massive scale, the creators of the Kyoto Station complex, which opened in 1997, did an excellent job of adding a modern structure to this traditional city. At 15 storeys, it is one of the tallest structures in town, yet it is not tall enough to intrude on Kyoto's natural cityscape of mountains and open skies. Also, despite its cavernous, breathtaking interiors (which include a broad, mountainside-like 171-step staircase, where a running race is held each year), this massive building does not overwhelm when viewed from the outside. Its external shape changes at city-block-sized

intervals, making the station look like a neat row of contemporary structures rather than a single imposing monolith of dark glass. It hearkens back to the machiya sensibility of a large building modestly concealing its true dimensions. Containing a theatre, an enormous 11-storey branch of the Isetan department store, numerous restaurants and the Hotel Granvia Kyoto, the train station building is a destination in its own right. It emphasises that Kyoto is an exciting, living city of the present, and not merely a museum of the past.

mona lisa in a temple

Kyoto's name literally means 'Capital Metropolis' (Tokyo means 'Eastern Capital') and its claim on the capital designation dates back to 794, when Emperor Kammu moved his government here in a bid to escape the political influence of Buddhist temples in nearby Nara, which had become Japan's first unified national capital in 710. Emperors would continue to live in Kyoto for more than a millennium, until 1868, although de facto political power would follow different shogunal dynasties away to Kamakura from 1192–1333 and to Edo (Tokyo) from 1603 onward.

In light of the reason for Kammu's move, it is mildly ironic that temples now dominate any list of Kyoto landmarks. Kinkakuji, Ginkakuji, Kiyomizudera and Ryoanji are four historic temples that usually occupy the top slots, each being famous for its landscaping, architecture or views.

A fifth temple, and said to be Kyoto's oldest, Koryuji has a beautiful garden but is better known for its famous occupant—a bodhisattva statue Miroku Bosatsu, aptly nicknamed the 'Mona Lisa of the Far East'. The soft smile on the face of this 1,400-year-old wooden statue hovers mysteriously between bliss and mirth. The delicate fingers of one hand seem to flutter near its cheek—but are they moving toward the face to cover an impending laugh, or is the head abruptly rising from the hand, where it had rested in thought?

THIS PAGE: *The South Court bar at the Hotel Granvia has some of the best views in Kyoto.*

OPPOSITE (FROM LEFT): *The grand and cavernous interior of Kyoto Station stretches on for blocks; another unique angle on the station's intriguing architecture.*

This bodhisattva figure is the highlight of a collection of Buddhist statuary on display. Kyoto's establishment as Japan's capital marked the start of the Heian period (794–1185), which is considered a golden age of high culture during which expressive woodcarving flourished. Many pieces of the Koryuji collection come from that time. The collection also includes a 13th-century statue of Prince Shotoku, who is said to have founded Koryuji in 603. A real-life historical figure and also the subject of many legends based on his wisdom, Shotoku is depicted at the young age of 16, sitting on a throne from which his feet do not reach the floor. He is shown with childish, chubby cheeks, but has a very serious expression on his face.

the world's most famous rocks

If asked to imagine a Zen garden, most people would visualise a perfectly flat rectangular field of white gravel, carefully raked around some large black rocks. Chances are, they would be thinking of the archetypical rock garden found at Ryoanji. These simple elements, arranged just so, hold endless mystery and fascination. One mystery is the question of who designed this garden. Its 15-by-31-m- (49-by-102-ft-) gravel bed is just a small part of Ryoanji; the 48-hectare (120-acre) complex actually includes several other gardens, more than a dozen buildings, and a large reflecting pond. It came into being as an aristocrat's country villa, and was converted to a Zen temple in 1450. It was around that time that the famous rock garden was installed, but little more is known about its origins.

THIS PAGE: Ryoanji temple's famous rock garden provides for a contemplative moment.
OPPOSITE (FROM TOP): Buddhist statuary depicts a range of symbolic hand gestures; the characters on this water basin at Ryoanji form an acrostic that can be read, 'I learn only to be contented'.

The garden's meaning is just as mysterious. There are 15 black rocks arranged in five groups, and what they stand for—if anything—is anyone's guess. The number 15 is thought to represent perfection or completeness, possibly because the Buddhist world is said to comprise seven continents and eight oceans, or possibly because it takes 15 days for a new moon to become full. One school of thought likens the five groups to Buddha, a whale, a tiger, a turtle and a bird, assigning a different symbolic value to each rock.

The rock garden is bordered by a mottled wall made of clay mixed with oil, and behind that wall rise about a dozen trees—each a different species, making for a great variety of foliage. This is a textbook example of the Japanese garden design concept of borrowed scenery—something outside the garden that enhances the experience of being inside it. Moreover, the passing breezes and changing seasons mean the leafy trees never look exactly the same from one moment to the next, while the rocks never change from one century to the next. But what that means is up to you.

pavilions of silver and gold

In 1397, the shogun Yoshimitsu Ashikaga began work on a villa northwest of Kyoto that would centre on a fabulous three-storey pavilion and be covered in gold leaf. His grandson, the shogun Yoshimasa Ashikaga, began work in the 1460s on a villa northeast of the city that would feature a dazzling two-storey pavilion covered in silver leaf. Today you can visit both of these dreamy retreats—but they are not exactly as they were in the beginning.

Each place was converted to a temple upon its respective shogun's death. The golden pavilion of Kinkakuji stood beside its tranquil reflecting pond for many centuries, until a mentally unbalanced monk burned it to the ground in 1950. Architecture's loss was literature's gain, as the incident inspired Yukio Mishima's 1956 novel, *The Temple of the Golden Pavilion*. The temple has been lovingly restored so that visitors can still see it as it was, even if the original is lost forever.

As for the silver pavilion at Ginkakuji, it is actually made of wood. Yoshimasa's misrule led to civil war and financial ruin, and his pavilion—despite its lustrous name—never received the intended silver coat. Yoshimasa stayed in his retreat while the wars worsened and Kyoto was destroyed around him. A peaceful sanctuary for him, its darkened, weather-beaten wood should inspire feelings of sabi, a Japanese aesthetic mood that encompasses a bittersweet appreciation of picturesque decay, but even Japanese visitors can be heard to exclaim in disappointment at the building's lack of glitter.

The real treasure at Ginkakuji, and one enjoyed by Yoshimasa, is on the ground. Claimed to have been designed by the great painter and landscape artist, Soami, the landscaping around the pavilion does wonders with raked sand, including a Fuji-esque flat-topped cone about 1 m (3¼ ft) high. There are also at least 48 varieties of moss cultivated beneath the trees on a shady hillside nearby. The garden covers a very large area, but the path through it is so winding that you can only see a little bit of it at a time—a waterfall here, a forest clearing there. This large garden, like so much in Kyoto, can only be appreciated on an intimate scale.

THIS PAGE: The pagoda at Kiyomizudera stands almost precariously on a hillside overlooking the ancient capital.

OPPOSITE (FROM TOP): Temple visitors leave prayers written on small wooden boards called ema; Japanese schoolgirls taste the fresh water at Kiyomizudera's venerable spring.

the pure water temple

The most famous of all Kyoto's temples, however, is better known for sweeping vistas than intimate glimpses. This is Kiyomizudera, literally the 'Pure Water Temple', founded in 788 by a Nara priest named Enchin who was looking for a fountain of pure water he had seen in a dream. From its humble beginnings beside a spring on a forested mountainside east of town, Kiyomizudera has grown over the years to a sprawling complex with a commanding view of the city.

Its largest and most unusual structure is a main hall, 57 m (187 ft) wide and 16 m (52½ ft) tall, that houses a kannon boddhisatva statue carved by Enchin himself. The statue is rarely on public display, but the hall still draws thousands of daily visitors to say a prayer or take in the scene. One attraction is the hall's remarkable position on a platform jutting out from the mountainside, supported by a wooden trestle of 139 pillars standing nearly as tall as the building itself. The platform and surrounding hillside paths are good places from which to admire the temple's towering three-tiered pagoda, standing against a dramatic backdrop of the city spread out below.

It's not rare for Buddhist temples in Japan to have a Shinto shrine on their grounds, and behind the main hall of Kiyomizudera you will find a shrine to the Shinto deity Okuninushino-mikoto, who is roughly equivalent to Cupid. In a statue at the entrance, he stands with his messenger—a large rabbit—by his side.

Downhill from these buildings is the sacred spring itself. Its water has been channelled into three streams that flow over the roof of a portico before falling into a stone-lined pond. Pilgrims and visitors lining up beneath the portico are given long-handled cups with which to reach out and intercept some of the falling water for a drink.

traditional craft items

The battered metal cups at the sacred fountain are reused continuously, but the Kiyomizudera neighbourhood is full of much nicer ceramic cups you can take home—not to mention bowls, platters and other examples of the potter's art. Two of the main

streets leading downhill from the temple, Kiyomizu-zaka and Chawan-zaka (the latter name means Tea Bowl Slope) are lined with dozens of tiny pottery shops selling everything from 200-yen chopstick rests to million-yen vases. A third street, Gojo-zaka, cuts across these two and is the site of the Gojo-zaka Pottery Festival each August.

If the pottery here offers a feast for the eyes, other nearby shops appeal to the nose—some offering delicate incense, and others touting aromatic Kyoto-style pickled vegetables. There are even shops for the skin, which may be cooled with a folding fan of paper or silk, or pampered with the creations of venerable cosmetician Yojiya.

Still more traditional craft items can be found in the Gion neighbourhood, just north of Kiyomizudera at the eastern end of bustling Shijo-dori. This area is home to the Kyoto Museum of Contemporary Art, the Minami-za kabuki theatre, several wagashi confectionery shops, and the Kyoto Craft Center, a 30-year-old cooperative run by Kyoto artisans offering a wide array of hand-crafted goods, most of which are small enough to be practical souvenirs.

A newer and more upscale version of the same thing can be found in the middle of the city at the Kyoto Traditional Craft Center, which opened in 2003 on Karasuma-dori. This features a wide range of chic and unique items, including furniture, made with traditional methods but in radically contemporary styles. A plus at this facility is an open studio where you can watch craftspeople at work.

A quick overview of classic Japanese art and design can be had at the Kyoto National Museum. Its layout is not the most creative, but the pieces themselves are still of interest. The collection begins with the prehistoric Jomon period (13,000–300 BCE), when the earliest distinctively Japanese designers created clay pots with basket-like textures by pressing ropes into their surface before firing them. Then come more widely known categories of artefacts, such as swords, kimonos, lacquerware and scrolls. One piece worth a special look is the life-size 14th-century statue of an elderly Buddhist priest named Itchin, who seems strong but tired and looks realistic enough to breathe. There are also antiquities from China and elsewhere.

The main building of the museum, reserved for special exhibits, was built in the 1890s in the French 'Neo-Renaissance' style typical of Meiji period buildings. A triangular frieze supported by columns above the entrance shows Buddhist deities depicted in what the museum calls a 'Graeco-Oriental manner'. Surrounded by statuary-filled gardens, this elegant old building makes for an impressive view from the Hyatt Regency Kyoto directly across the street, especially when illuminated in the evenings.

a culture shaped by women

Visitors to the Kiyomizudera area are often delighted to catch a glimpse of a geisha shuffling prettily down the street in wooden platform sandals, face powder, a brightly coloured kimono and an enormous black wig. Chances are, this person is actually a maiko, or geisha in training. Maiko are a regular part of the local scenery, but older, fully-fledged geisha tend to be more elusive. All across the city, however, you will notice ordinary women going about their daily business in traditional dress—albeit in less elaborate forms than geisha or maiko wear. You may see dozens of kimono on the streets of Kyoto in a single day, while in Tokyo it is sometimes possible to go a dozen days without seeing one. Men in kimono are rarer still.

If women are the most visible keepers of traditional culture, it is only fitting. Indeed, it can be said that women created much of Japan's high culture. In the golden age of the Heian period, ladies of the Kyoto court produced two of the most important works of classic Japanese literature: *The Pillow Book* by Sei Shonagon and *The Tale of Genji* by Murasaki Shikibu.

THIS PAGE (FROM TOP): Japanese swords, hand-crafted reminders of another time in history; the deliberate simplicity of this private dining room at Touzan, Hyatt Regency Kyoto adds to the authentic experience. OPPOSITE: Elaborate embroidery is displayed at one of the many festivals on Kyoto's calendar.

The latter work has inspired numerous film, TV and animation adaptations, and an old illustration of one of its scenes appears on the back of the 2,000 yen note.

An equally great contribution was made by a woman named Okuni in 1603. In that year, this shrine attendant led a group of performers in a comedy and dance show played out on a stage sitting on the dry bed of the Kamo River. It was so far from ordinary that it led to the creation of a whole new theatrical genre—kabuki.

Cultural creativity, however, does not always translate into real power, and the government eventually decreed that only men could perform in kabuki shows, a restriction that is observed to this day.

kaiseki and the way of tea

The tea ceremony is a refined cultural activity originally developed by men—most notably the 16th-century Kyoto master Sen no Rikyu—that nowadays is more often practised by women. But anyone may participate in this sedate ritual, which embodies the Kyoto spirit of slowing down to carefully appreciate the aesthetic aspects of life. A tea ceremony is an intimate occasion during which a skilled master prepares the frothy green beverage for a small group of guests. Everything is done very slowly, the better to appreciate the beauty of the ceramic bowls, the bamboo implements, the quiet atmosphere and—at last—the tea itself. The slightly bitter drink is accompanied by mildly sweet wagashi, confections made primarily from beans and rice. Wagashi are tiny works of art carefully shaped to represent seasonal motifs such as flowers and leaves, and sometimes they will even come wrapped in a real leaf.

It's all quite exquisite, but not very filling. For that reason, some tea masters prepared light meals for their guests, called kaiseki. These simple repasts gradually evolved to mark the height of elegance and refinement in traditional cuisine. Kaiseki meals are now usually enjoyed on their own, without a tea ceremony.

True to its roots, the portions in kaiseki are dainty, but there tend to be many of them. The food must be of the very best quality and appropriate to the season, and its

THIS PAGE (FROM TOP): *Tea ceremony utensils include a bamboo whisk; a woman wears a look of concentration while practising the tea ceremony.*

OPPOSITE (FROM LEFT): *Traditional beauty requires constant upkeep even while sleeping; maiko, or apprentice geisha, are known for their especially flamboyant kimono.*

presentation is given equal importance. Each morsel is shown off to its best advantage on its own carefully chosen tray, dish or bowl. An edible garnish might be as simple, but as surprising, as a single fermented bean skewered on a fresh pine needle. A feast for the eyes as well as the palate, kaiseki is a work of art, meant to be savoured slowly.

Kyoto is home to the nation's best-known kaiseki chef and artist, Yoshihiro Murata. A magazine columnist, star of his own TV cooking show, and author of several books, Murata comes from a long line of chefs but has earned his fame in his own right. Stunningly creative yet faithfully traditional, the dishes at his Kikunoi restaurants in Kyoto and Tokyo are a roaring success. In one example, an autumn dish he calls Planked Barracuda, the seasonally fatty, marinated fish is topped with shiitake mushrooms and bound between two thin planks of cedar, which the chef sets alight with a propane torch. The dish is literally smouldering as it is placed before the customer.

Kyoto plays host to many other famous kaiseki restaurants; one such establishment is Hyo-tei. More than 300 years old, Hyo-tei is made up of a cluster of teahouses and is located near the Heian Shrine, where the ambience of a lush garden surroundings enhances the delicacy of the meal. Here you may sample the work of Chef Eiichi Takahashi and his son Yoshihiro, whose dishes include a meal they call Asagayu. Beginning with simple okayu (rice porridge), a traditional Japanese comfort food, side dish after side dish are added until this common childhood favourite becomes a sophisticated and grown-up feast.

Chef Kunio Tokuoka achieves a similar transition from the everyday to the elegant in his chain of restaurants Kyoto Kitcho. There are several branches, including one located in the Hotel Granvia at Kyoto Station that sells top-notch bento boxed meals. In Japan, even the ubiquitous and cheap bento that are available at convenience stores may include an intriguing array of items, and Japanese mothers make an art out of packing home-cooked goodies in bento boxes for their children to take to school. Kyoto Kitcho,

THIS PAGE (FROM LEFT): Individual serving trays line a tatami-floored dining room at Kikunoi; Chef Murata checks for flavour.

OPPOSITE (FROM TOP): A tiny cricket cage filled with autumn delicacies form an elegant food presentation by Chef Murata; cherry blossoms explode outside of Kikunoi's windows.

however, successfully transforms the quotidian bento concept and brings it into the realm of haute cuisine, arranging about 20 kaiseki-style items in each ready-to-go box. It's just the thing for a cherry blossom party or riverside picnic.

For those who would rather eat indoors, the main branch of Kyoto Kitcho serves Chef Tokuoka's kaiseki creations on 400-year-old plates in private rooms with garden views in the city's northwestern Arashiyama area. Tokuoka is a grandson of the restaurant's original chef, and the antique tableware is one sign that he understands the value of tradition. But he also looks to expand his horizons, saying: "Today, as various kinds of ingredients are gathered from all over the world, new styles and methods of cookery are being created and developed, resulting in the continuing evolution of cooking as an art." This approach to cuisine may explain why he was lauded by *The New York Times* in 2005 and named chef of the year by *GQ Japan* magazine in 2006.

the retail rectangle

Once dominated by an imperial court that looked down upon lowly merchants, the retailers of downtown Kyoto are enjoying sweet revenge in modern times. A broad swathe of the city centre has become a shoppers' paradise. The epicentre of this retail revolution is a rectangle easily identifiable by the Kamo River located along the east, Karasuma-dori along the west, Oike-dori along the north and Shijo-dori along the south. Shijo-dori in particular is crammed to brimming with high-end shops, including the main Kyoto branches of the Daimaru and Takashimaya department store chains. International brands such as Benetton, Gap, Emporio Armani, and of course Louis Vuitton all have Kyoto stores, mostly situated in this area, which is also home to various little galleries and boutiques. And, as in any big Japanese city, Starbucks is virtually ubiquitous, to say nothing of fast-food establishments.

BELOW: The bright lights of an ancient city shine on Shijo-dori, one of Kyoto's up-to-the-minute shopping streets.

OPPOSITE: Now as in centuries past, portrait prints of geisha are popular Kyoto mementos.

But for the more refined palate, there's no shortage of options for a more distinctively Kyoto-style meal in this area. At Nakamura, a restaurant in an old machiya house with a traditionally tiny garden near Oike-dori, sixth-generation chef Motokazu Nakamura serves Steamed Sushi in a basket, along with other specialities. Tankuma Kitamise is a newer restaurant, at least by Kyoto standards. It dates back to 1928, and has counted the novelist Junichiro Tanizaki (1886–1965) among its regular customers. It's near the Takase River, actually a small stream that parallels the Kamo River at the eastern end of the rectangle. Chef Masahiro Kurisu specialises in dishes of river fish, as many restaurateurs in the area once did. Just past the retail rectangle's western end, near Karasuma-dori, is Kinobu, where third-generation chef Takuji Takahashi is a licensed wine sommelier and also a kikizakeshi—essentially a sake sommelier. He is highly qualified to pair his kaiseki dishes with either Western wine or Japanese sake.

The nationwide shopping mall renaissance has touched Karasuma-dori in the form of two attractive new retail venues. Shoppers who like the Queen Victoria Building in Sydney or Georgetown Park in Washington will feel at home in the Shin Puh Kan, a mall that opened in 2001 with its modern interior hidden behind the red-brick façade of a 1920s telephone exchange building. A few blocks away, Cocon Karasuma takes a less modest approach, with its hip frontage of painted glass brilliantly illuminated at night.

Bisecting the retail rectangle is Teramachi-dori, which has been converted into a roofed, pedestrian-only shopping arcade six blocks long from north to south. A similar arcade runs parallel to it one block east, while another branches off to run six blocks west. It's possible to spend countless hours on these indoor streets, shopping for art, cloth, antiques, stationery, jewellery, manga comics, hanko seals and more. The street gets its name from the fact that it was once lined with temples (tera), a few of which still exist. At the northern end of the shopping arcade stands the modern incarnation of Honnoji temple, which was burned to the ground shortly after the warlord Oda Nobunaga was forced to commit suicide there in 1582.

THIS PAGE (FROM TOP): A DJ calls the tune at a Kyoto nightclub; this young Kyoto woman knows that a kimono is not the only way to look good for a night out on the town.

OPPOSITE: The lanterns come on as dusk settles over an old-fashioned Kyoto side street.

Near the southern end of the Teramachi arcade stands Opa, a conglomerate department store in the style of Tokyo's 109. This is where Kyoto's au courant 20-somethings go to keep their cutting-edge honed. In contrast to the city's usual air of understated charm, the staff and shoppers here are young and gorgeous and want you to know it. Few over the age of 30 could keep up with this relentlessly glam crowd. Jewellery and accessories are sold at some of the counters, but most specialise in trendy or even pre-trendy clothing.

Located just northeast of the rectangle, Kyoto's trendy parade their purchases in nightclubs such as Metro. Dating from the 1990s, Metro is one of Japan's longest-running nightclubs. It is famous as the launching pad of DJ duo Kyoto Jazz Massive, who are now a leading force on the music scene nationwide. While Metro may be the city's most important contemporary music club, it is far from the only one, with venues such as World and Lab.Tribe also attracting night owls in the know.

...most specialise in trendy or even pre-trendy clothing.

Hyatt Regency Hakone Resort + Spa

Surrounded by beautiful scenery, relaxing onsen, mountainous walks and fresh country air, Hakone, in the Kanagawa prefecture, is a popular weekend resort for Tokyoites. Conveniently located 80 km (43 miles) west of Tokyo, the journey takes only 30 minutes on the bullet train and 40 minutes by car from the city, making Hakone an ideal daytrip destination.

Amid the greenery of the popular Fuji Hakone Izu National Park, Hyatt Regency Hakone Resort and Spa has created a luxurious escape from the crowded space of the city. Incorporating a spa, stylish restaurants and boutique-style guestrooms, this hotel resort is a chic little hideaway. Visitors can relax on their private sun terrace, take a leisurely stroll in the surrounding countryside or indulge in the natural onsen.

The guestrooms are close to 68 sq m (732 sq ft) in size. Designed as self-contained residences, their contemporary style blends immaculately with the surrounding nature. From the balcony, guests can feel part of the scenery with a view that looks out across the breathtaking mountainous area and the dramatic stature of Mount Fuji. Technology is not forgotten, as high-speed Internet access, large plasma TVs, DVD and CD players are available in every room. Yet, given such peace and natural beauty, it is perhaps unsurprising should guests choose to overlook these gadgets and pick up a good book for a relaxing read instead. Both Western- and Japanese-designed rooms contain deluxe beds or traditional tatami mats, and bathrooms feature overflowing bathtubs with a surrounding wet area and powerful rain

showers. For a little pooch pampering, several rooms even pander to guests' dogs with a separate pet shower room.

With the nearest restaurants some 20 minutes away, most guests choose to have their meals at the hotel, where a selection of stylish dining rooms provide both local and Western delicacies. A French brasserie, Dining Room serves delicious Japanese cuisine as well, complete with a sushi counter and an outdoor terrace. Living Room owns a huge open fireplace where guests can enjoy a hot drink, or simply relax, by the crackling fire during winter. Wine connoisseurs will be pleased to know that Living Room also serves as a sophisticated and cosy den that offers an impressive selection of wines and sakes.

Like the natural healing environment of Hakone, Spa IZUMI is an onsen and wellness spa incorporating eight treatment rooms, each with a private mist sauna and bath, and two natural hot spring baths. Their unique Lunar Phase Treatment—a 28-day programme following the four stages of the moon to re-balance and regenerate the guest's mind and body—is the ultimate indulgence and a great booster to a healthy lifestyle. Providing convenience, Izumi Spa offers flexible seven-, three- and half-day, or 90- and 30-minute packages that feature relaxing head massages, facials, revitalising massages, foot soaks and body polishes, rounding off the perfect stay at the resort.

THIS PAGE: Sample Dining Room's excellent range of wines.

OPPOSITE (CLOCKWISE FROM LEFT): This hideaway retreat combines style with a peaceful charm; enjoy coffee or tea and relax in Living Room's cosy ambience; at Dining Room, diners get to enjoy authentic French and Japanese cuisine prepared with the finest ingredients from the Hakone region.

FACTS		
ROOMS	79	
FOOD	Dining Room: French and Japanese • Living Room: light meal and afternoon tea	
DRINK	Living Room	
FEATURES	Spa IZUMI • function room • company retreats • events	
NEARBY	Hakone Art Museum • Hakone Open-Air Museum • Lake Ashi • Owakudani Crater • Sengokuhara •	
CONTACT	1320 Gora Hakone-machi, Ashigarashimo-gun, Kanagawa, 250-0408 • telephone: +81.460.822 000 • facsimile: +81.460.822 001 • email: reservations.hakone@hyattintl.com • website: www.hakone.regency.hyatt.com	

PHOTOGRAPHS COURTESY OF HYATT REGENCY HAKONE RESORT + SPA.

Gora Kadan

According to the owner, her grandfather first bought the house and his wife converted it into a guesthouse in 1952. Being the excellent host, this hospitable lady provided a warm and cosy environment for her guests by personally tending to the flower arrangements and sewing a yukata, a casual kimono, for each of them.

After the elderly lady passed away, the family considered selling off the property, but as the owner could not bear to part with it, she took over and reopened the hotel in 1989. A new main building was then erected and Gora Kadan was born, becoming the welcoming and exquisite lodging it is today.

THIS PAGE (FROM TOP): *Gora Kadan's picturesque setting provides the ideal retreat away from the stress of the outside world; the Zen-like corridors lead to a calming experience for guests.*

OPPOSITE (FROM LEFT): *The soft colours of the hotel entrance set the tone for a relaxing time; view of the lush greenery from one of the guestrooms.*

Located within the lush forests of the popular Japanese attraction, Hakone National Park, Gora Kadan is a sublime ryokan. The name Gora Kadan—The Garden of Gora—came about as a result of the owner's grandmother's love for flowers. Surrounded by the peace and quiet of Mother Nature, the hotel enjoys a unique blend of modern sophistication with the richness of traditional Japanese style.

...a unique blend of modern sophistication with the richness of traditional Japanese style.

After a refreshing soak in the large tub, a special meal awaits. The most delectable kaiseki ryouri—kaiseki cuisine—is on offer. There is fresh fish from the Suruga and Sagami Bays, plus various seasonal ingredients from all over the archipelago. Remaining true to the basics of kaiseki, dishes are always served piping hot. With an itinerary that combines both relaxation and excellent cuisine, it is difficult to resist a return to Goran Kadan for another stay.

The view from the guestroom windows is the splendour of Myojyou-Ga-Take Mountain where the famous Daimonji can be seen; a Japanese character, Dai, is lit up on the slopes of the mountain during the annual summer festival. Drawn from a natural source, the outdoor communal hot spring bath eases away tension and is said to help neuralgia and rheumatism sufferers with its weak alkaline-based water. Just as relaxing is the unique gambanyoku, or bedrock bath, a germanium-based bed made of a single sheet of black silica that not only rejuvenates the skin, but also strengthens the immune system and helps increase the rate of metabolism.

FACTS	**ROOMS**	37
	FOOD	Kadan: kaiseki
	DRINK	Club Ai: karaoke • Lounge Hanakage • Salon Seiran
	FEATURES	fitness club • flower arrangement service • thermal hot bath • Internet • Kadan Spa • limousine • pool
	NEARBY	Gora Station • Hakone Museum of Art • Hakone open-air Museum • Lake Ashinoko
	CONTACT	1300 Gora Hakone-machi, Ashigara-shimogun, Kanagawa-ken, 250-0408 • telephone: +81.460.23331 • facsimile: +81.460.23334 • email: info@gorakadan.com • website: www.gorakadan.com

PHOTOGRAPHS COURTESY OF GORA KADAN.

Hotel Granvia Kyoto

THIS PAGE (FROM TOP): Stylish décor aside, high-speed Internet access is complimentary in all guestrooms; the chrome lighting and dark walls give the hotel lobby an avant-garde look.

OPPOSITE (CLOCKWISE FROM LEFT): The impressive and highly futuristic Kyoto Station Building; look forward to a comfortable stay at Hotel Granvia Kyoto; with an exclusive and cosy ambience, Shiokouji Rakusui offers Western- and Japanese-style dining rooms that are perfect for private functions.

With over 1,600 Buddhist temples interspersed with the city's sleek and modern buildings, Japan's ancient capital city, Kyoto, still retains its old-world charm, as much as it is a thriving commercial centre today.

Housed in the internationally acclaimed and highly futuristic Kyoto Station Building, Hotel Granvia Kyoto combines the city's rich past with all the trimmings of modern-day comfort to create a luxurious haven. The JR Kyoto Station is located just below, and major cities like Osaka, Nara and Tokyo are easily accessible. A shopping mall, numerous restaurants and the city's musical theatre are found inside the building, and Kyoto's major sightseeing attractions such as the Toji temples and beautiful Zen gardens are conveniently located nearby.

The hotel lobby is decorated in an artistic fashion, with its dark walls brightened by a beautiful display of six-fold traditional Japanese folding screens with an impressive showcase of grand Chinese-style pottery. Guestrooms offer a soothing ambience with soft colour tones, while the hotel's top quality beds ensure maximum comfort for guests.

There are 14 restaurants and bars in the hotel, out of which five are dedicated to authentic Japanese cuisine, which Kyoto is renowned for. The Granvia's impressive range of facilities also includes an indoor pool, sauna, jet bath and a beauty salon.

The hotel offers a range of unique cultural experiences that are not found in tourist guidebooks. Through the Ozashiki Asobi experience, the hotel can arrange for guests to enjoy the performances of geishas in a traditional teahouse setting, which is otherwise closed to the public. Japanese cookery classes are also conducted by a Master Chef who will teach guests the art of traditional Japanese cuisine such as kaiseki. Other interesting packages include visits to the inner sanctum of the Kamigamo Shrine, which are led by a Shinto priest. By offering rare glimpses into the esoteric world of Shintoism, such visits highlight the admirable coexistence shared between tradition and modernity that is very much the embodiment of Hotel Granvia Kyoto.

FACTS	
ROOMS	539
FOOD	Banzai • Gorairo • Gozanbo • Grace Garden • Kitcho • Kyorinsen • La Fleur • Le Temps • Roppongi Rogairo • Shiki • Shiokouji Rakusui • Ukihashi
DRINK	Grand Jour • Orbite • Southern Court
FEATURES	fitness and health facilities • Internet • pool • wedding facilities
NEARBY	Hongan-ji temples • Shoseien Garden • Kyoto Theatre • Kyoto Tower • JR Kyoto Station
CONTACT	901 Higashi-shiokoji-cho, Shiokoji-sagaru, Karasuma-dori, Shimogyo-ku, Kyoto, 600-8216 • telephone: +81.75.344 8888 • facsimile: +81.75.344 4400 • email: hotel@granvia-kyoto.co.jp • website: www.granvia-kyoto.co.jp/e/

PHOTOGRAPHS COURTESY OF HOTEL GRANVIA KYOTO.

Hyatt Regency Kyoto

THIS PAGE: *With natural colours and delicate Japanese kimono fabric, guestrooms provide both comfort and a Zen-like feel.*

OPPOSITE (FROM LEFT): *Enjoy a relaxing soak in the wooden bathtub while taking in the beautiful garden view; with its majestic décor, the lobby will make guests feel like royalty.*

Traditional and charming, the quaint district of Higashiyama Shichijo represents the cultural heart of Japan's ancient capital, Kyoto, where the city's oldest surviving buildings—that date back over a thousand years—and some of the most celebrated temples and gardens are found. Surrounded by bamboo trees and such picturesque setting of unspoilt greenery and history, Hyatt Regency Kyoto enjoys a superb location, catering to the luxurious comforts of the modern day at the same time.

In keeping with the Japanese sense of beauty and elegance, the hotel entrance and lobby are simply mesmerising. With backlit glass and pristine white metal, the

...enjoys a superb location, catering to the luxurious comforts of the modern day...

ceiling is decorated with openwork frames that are designed with traditional Japanese patterns. Ornate but exquisite details run down the glowing pillars, which in turn illuminate the room.

Blending contemporary Japanese sophistication with more traditional elements, guestrooms are each individually designed. Natural colours and white oak furniture create a calm and tranquil feel while large headboards made of amazingly rich kimono fabric form the perfect contrast with the neutral tones. Old wooden vases and other furniture decorate the room, adding to the warm and cosy feel. Rooms are also equipped with the latest entertainment technology that includes flat screen satellite TV, DVD player and Internet access. For the ultimate Japanese relaxation,

bathrooms feature a separate wet area with free-standing granite and a deep-soaking bath, definitely a luxurious way to unwind at the end of the day.

Gratifyingly indulgent, the hotel's suites —located on the first floor—overlook the traditional Japanese gardens, the waterfall and pond. In the bedroom, an oversized bed and a giant TV screen are bound to provide maximum comfort. The other side of a crawl-through doorway reveals a

hidden Japanese-style room, with modern tatami flooring and a sunken kotatsu table forming a fun living area. In addition to a wooden bathtub and granite flooring, the bathroom in the Deluxe Balcony room also offers a spectacular view of the gardens.

The hotel's spa, RIRAKU Spa and Fitness, has 10 treatment rooms including two spa suites, a steam room, sauna and gym. Highly trained consultants provide professional advice for training, diet,

THIS PAGE: *Enjoy prime cuts of meat and the freshest seafood at THE GRILL.*

OPPOSITE (FROM LEFT): *RIRAKU offers a wide range of programmes, providing a truly relaxing and indulging experience; guests can enjoy the beautiful view of the exquisite and peaceful Japanese gardens from their suites.*

health and wellness issues and the use of Japanese medicine. Employing traditional and modern methods, RIRAKU presents a wide range of programmes including shiatsu, acupuncture and aromatherapy. Spa treatments begin with an uplifting footbath that contains local sake, followed by the traditional Kyoto-style okiyome—incense powder—treatment, designed to stimulate all five senses and to help re-balance mind, body and soul.

After two and a half hours of pampering, the KOMACHI treatment will leave guests feeling rejuvenated. Starting with an invigorating full-body exfoliation using essential oils that relieve tired and aching muscles, the deep body massage—with Japanese mint salt that works right into the joints—that follows leaves the body feeling restored. As for the NENE spa package, traditional Kyoto camellia and azuki beans are used to moisturise, nourish and tone the skin. After a facial and full-body massage, a final head, hand and arm massage would leave guests feeling completely revitalised.

Kyoto is said to be home to some of Japan's most refined cuisine, one of which is kaiseki, the traditional Japanese style. Adding to the local fare are varieties from across the country as well as international influences, creating an abundance of both Japanese and Western gastronomic delights all within easy reach of the hotel. The hotel also offers its own selection of exciting dishes in three unique settings. Beautifully rustic and Japanese, Touzan is modelled after traditional Kyoto-style houses. Slightly parted rattan blinds hang across the windows, allowing diners to look out and marvel at the Zen gardens. Glass lanterns suspended from the ceiling create a spectacular sight while the elegantly carved wooden chairs make very comfortable seats. Separated

...an abundance of both Japanese and Western gastronomic delights...

At THE GRILL, prime cuts of meat are served, and chefs whip up the freshest seafood, as evident from the aromas wafting out from the open kitchen and wood-burning ovens. The restaurant boasts an impressive wine cellar, stocking wines from all over the world, while its contemporary Japanese décor is just as inspiring. The stunning lobby ceiling extends into the restaurant, creating a dramatic visual impact against the glass walls that overlook the Japanese gardens.

Indeed, Kyoto is an attractive city and while the hotel does offer luxurious products and services, it is also ideally situated for guests to make the most of the city's main attractions and take in its spectacular sights. Many temples are located nearby, such as Kiyomizudera. One of the most recognised in Japan, the historic Kiyomizudera will not disappoint with breathtaking views of the city from its famous 1,200-year-old wooden verandah. On the eastern bank of the Kamogawa River lies the Gion District,

where geishas can be spotted walking down the lanes that are lined with traditional buildings and teahouses. If venturing out of the city is on the itinerary, the JR Kyoto Station is only a few minutes drive away, from where the train will take visitors to Osaka, Nara and Tokyo.

from the main restaurant by a glass partition decorated with antique tiles is the unique sushi bar that serves mouth-watering charcoal grills and fresh sushi with a wide variety of premium sake.

Trattoria sette offers home-style Italian dishes and crisp, Neapolitan pizzas in a casual trattoria-style setting with heavy wooden floorboards and rough sandstone walls. From the warm and cosy ambience, diners can sit back, relax and observe the adjoining pastry boutique, bustling espresso bar and the beautiful Japanese garden.

FACTS

ROOMS	189
FOOD	THE GRILL: steak and seafood • Touzan: Japanese • trattoria sette: Italian
DRINK	Touzan Bar
FEATURES	ancient Japanese garden • RIRAKU Spa and Fitness • function rooms • wedding facilities • banquet rooms
NEARBY	Kiyomizudera • Sanjusangendo • Chishakuin • Tofukuji and Sennyuji temples • Gion District • Kyoto National Museum • JR Kyoto Station
CONTACT	644-2 Sanjusangendo-mawari, Higashiyama-ku, Kyoto, 6050941 • telephone: +81.75.541 1234 • facsimile: +81.75.541 2203 • e-mail: info@hyattregencykyoto.com • website: www.kyoto.regency.hyatt.com

PHOTOGRAPHS COURTESY OF HYATT REGENCY KYOTO.

Yojiya

Specialist cosmetics company, Yojiya, first opened its doors way back in 1904 in Japan's ancient capital, Kyoto. Its founders originally sold cosmetic goods from pushcarts before deciding to set up shop in central Kyoto. Since then, Yojiya has gained a reputation for producing quality cosmetics, and it was their ability to keep up with the ever-changing needs of consumers that has helped Yojiya establish itself as the leading cosmetics brand on the market.

Creating unique products that are said to enhance the natural beauty of women, Yojiya cosmetics are extremely popular among Japanese women who buy from the diverse range of products. The best-selling product is aburatorigami, or oil-blotting facial paper, with origins that can be traced back to 1920. Instantly recognised by its trademark 'Yojiya face'—a reflection of a woman's face on a hand mirror—on the packaging, aburatorigami made Yojiya the popular brand it is today. After the pocketbook-sized version was introduced, aburatorigami quickly became a hit, especially among Kyoto's actresses and those working within the city's entertainment industry. News of this reputable facial-

THIS PAGE (CLOCKWISE FROM TOP): With a rich history, Yojiya has become the standard bearer of quality cosmetic products; Yojiya's aburatorigami is available in the limited edition of aloe, cherry blossom and citrus varieties; enjoy a fresh brew at the cafés.

OPPOSITE (FROM LEFT): The cafés serve desserts that taste as good as they look; the company sells a wide range of cosmetic goods.

...a household brand that is synonymous with Kyoto.

material, a special paper that is actually a by-product of traditional gold-leaf. As pure gold is beaten into a thin leaf, the supporting paper is also beaten out. Today, Yojiya uses handmade Japanese paper and a gold beating machine. The beating activates the fine texture of the paper creating the perfect facial-blotter for a mild and velvety sensation on the skin.

Yojiya has 11 outlets in Kyoto, the main one in Shinkyogoku, and three in the airports of Tokyo and Osaka. In the shops, guests are able to choose from Yojiya's wide selection of cosmetic products. Beauty aside, Yojiya also runs three cafés in and around Kyoto. In Sanjo, the Yojiya café has a casual dining atmosphere in which guests can enjoy pastas and desserts. Housed in traditional Japanese homes, the other two cafés in Sagano-Arashiyama and Ginkakuji are located within the premises of the retail outlets, where guests can enjoy original sweets.

blotter soon reached every corner of Japan, and the Yojiya brand has been a common feature in fashion magazines ever since. It is now considered a household brand that is synonymous with Kyoto.

The reason why aburatorigami took off the way it did and why it has become such a coveted cosmetic product lies in its

FACTS

PRODUCTS	cosmetics • aburatorigami facial paper
FEATURES	cafés • online shopping
NEARBY	Ginkakuji temple • Gion district • Kinkakuji temple • Kiyomizu temple • Kyoto Station • Ponto-cho • Sagano Arashiyama • Sanjo Street • Shinkyogoku • Tenryuji temple
CONTACT	538 Ichinofunairi-cho, Nijo-sagaru, Kawaramachi-dori, Nakagyo-ku, Kyoto, 604-0924 • telephone: +81.75.253 1707 • facsimile: +81.75.253 1708 • email: info@yojiya.co.jp • website: www.yojiya.co.jp

PHOTOGRAPHS COURTESY OF YOJIYA.

Japan Airlines

Japan Airlines (JAL) has grown to be the largest carrier in the Asia-Pacific region and the world's third largest airline in operating revenue. Today the fleet numbers some 270 aircraft. With a network spanning the globe serving 35 countries and territories, over 215 airports and over 243 international routes, JAL connects Japan to the rest of the world. Flights link Tokyo and Osaka to 77 destinations in the US and over 20 cities across Europe. In addition, JAL operates the largest Japanese domestic network, linking 61 airports with 166 routes.

Having just joined the ONEWORLD airline alliance, JAL's worldwide connections have substantially increased with smooth flight transfers, ticketing and competitive fares across some 700 destinations in nearly 150 countries. Recently voted the world's leading alliance, together with carriers American Airlines, British Airways, Cathay Pacific, Finnair, Iberia, LAN, Malev, Qantas and Royal Jordanian, JAL now offers travellers a range of global travel options and benefits that are unsurpassed.

For eligible travellers, JAL's international lounges provide a restful haven where they can await their flight in comfort. Guests can also enjoy complimentary light snacks and drinks, showers and business facilities including Internet access and computer terminals.

On board it is JAL's attention to detail and high standard of customer service across all classes that make all the difference. Passengers in all classes enjoy a delicious choice of Japanese or Western cuisine accompanied by complimentary wines, sake or choice of other alcoholic or soft drinks. Additional snacks and beverages are supplied throughout the flight at the Sky Oasis self-service corner. International passengers are entertained with the 'MAGIC' AVOD (audio/video on demand) system that offers a wide selection of films, music and games accessible at their

THIS PAGE: Its excellent schedules and comfortable flights have made Japan Airlines a popular choice among travellers.

OPPOSITE (FROM LEFT): Flat bed-style seats ensure JAL First and Executive Class Seasons passengers arrive at their destinations well refreshed; a smooth flight is enhanced by the professional and warm service of the crew.

Travellers are always treated as special guests whenever they fly JAL.

convenience. For Business and First Class passengers, this entertainment experience is enhanced by noise cancelling headphones.

With the JAL Shell Flat Seat—one of the largest in its class—those travelling in the Executive Class Seasons cabin are ensured a comfortable journey. There is a built-in massage function and the seat reclines to any position at the touch of a button. Japanese meals aside, passengers can

choose from the delectable European 'Escoffier' menu that is carefully prepared under the guidance of the Association des Disciples D'Auguste Escoffier du Japon, an association of chefs from Japan's finest French restaurants.

First Class passengers will be able to indulge in the JAL Skysleeper Solo Seat, which is upholstered in luxurious cream leather by Poltrona Frau of Italy—one of

the world's leading furniture makers—and reclines with a massage function to ensure a restful journey. With only 11 seats in this cabin, each one offers plenty of privacy for a truly relaxing and enjoyable flight.

Travellers are always treated as special guests whenever they fly JAL. Whether travelling on business or for leisure, whatever the class of travel, JAL gets everyone's Japan experience off to the best possible start.

FACTS

FLIGHTS	35 countries • 216 airports
IN FLIGHT	Personal audio/video on demand entertainment system with films, music and games • Western or Japanese cuisine • complimentary alcoholic and soft drinks including wine and sake • reading material • duty-free shopping First Class and Executive Class Seasons: 'flat bed-style' seats with built-in massage function • à la carte menu on-demand
GROUND CONTACT	First Class and Executive Class Seasons lounges UK reservations: 0845 774 7700 • Japan: 0120 25 5931 • website: www.jal.com

PHOTOGRAPHS COURTESY OF JAPAN AIRLINES.

index

picturecredits+acknowledgements

The publisher would like to thank the following for permission to reproduce their photographs:

Angelo Hornak/Corbis 32 (left)
B.S.P.I./Corbis 92, 168, 184 (right)
Badou-R front cover (shirts)
Barry Cronin/Zuma/Corbis 99 (below)
Beige Alain Ducasse Tokyo 44 (top + below)
Bela/Photolibrary 106 (top)
Bettmann/Corbis 15 (top)
Catherine Karnow/Corbis 198 (below)
Cheryl Fan 35 (top), 191 (top)
Christian Kober/Photolibrary 108
Christian Kober/Corbis 106 (below), 182 (below)
Conor Hehir 43 (top), 45 (below)
Conrad Tokyo front cover (restaurant), back flap (right), 47
DAJ Digital Images/Disc 075 back cover (folded kimono), front flap (tent),14 (top), 175 (centre + below), 181 (below), 187 (below), 189 (left)
Dallas + John Heaton/Free Agents Limited/Corbis 174
Dave Bartruff/Photolibrary 176 (left)
David Sanger/Photodisc Red/Getty Images 187 (top)
Demetrio Carrasco/Photolibrary 23
Dresscamp back cover (dress), 104
Ed Freeman/Getty Images 199
Envision/Corbis front cover (green tea), 193 (top)
Everett Kennedy Brown/EPA/Corbis 51 (top)
Fukumitsuya Sake Brewery 45 (top)
Gavin Hellier/JAI/Corbis 43 (below)
Glen Allison/Getty Images front cover (busy street), 12
Grand Hyatt Tokyo back cover (suite)
Grant Faint/Getty Images 26
Hakone Open-Air Museum 177
Haruyoshi Yamaguchi/Corbis 36 (below)
Hiroshi Watanabe/Getty Images 15 (below)
Hiroyuki Matsumoto/Getty Images 180
Historical Picture Archive/Corbis 18 (top)
Hotel Granvia Kyoto 185

Hyatt Regency Hakone 176 (right)
Hyatt Regency Kyoto back flap (top), back cover (screen), front flap (below), 191 (below)
Issey Miyake Aoyama 115
Jacob Halaska/Photolibrary 2
Japan Airlines 42
Japan National Tourist Organization 31 (above), 175 (top)
Jeffrey L. Rotman/Corbis 34 (top)
Jerry Driendl/Getty Images 97 (below), 196–197 (below)
Jesper Haynes/On Asia 111 (top)
Joey Nigh/Corbis 41 (right)
John Dakers/Eye Ubiquitous/Corbis 32 (right)
JTB Photo Communications Inc./Photolibrary 28, 38, 39, 112 (top), 170, 182 (top)
Justin Guariglia/National Geographic Image Collection 30 (top) 95, 101 (below), 105 (right), 107, 110, 188, 189 (below)
Karen Kasmauski/National Geographic Image Collection 173 (below), 192 (left)
Karin Slade/Getty Images 46
Kathy Collins/Getty Images 172, 173 (above)
Lalique Museum Hakone 179 (centre)
Lisa Damayanti 22 above, 52 (below), 183
Lynn Chen 20 (top)
Mark Gresham 33 (top) 40 (top)
Masashi Kuma, from the book *Kaiseki*, courtesy of Yoshihiro Murata + Kodansha International Ltd front cover (sashimi + cherry blossom), 6, 24 (above + below), 35 (below), 190, 194 (top + below) 195, (top + below)
Matthias Clamer/Getty Images front cover (window seat), 13
Michael S. Yamashita/Corbis 14 (below), 17 right, 22 (below), 50, 99 (top), 186, 192 (right), 193 (below)
Michael S. Yamashita/National Geographic Image Collection 172 (below)
Miramax/Bureau L.A. Collection/Corbis 17 (left)
Mizuma Art Gallery 112 (centre), 113 (left)

Mori Building Co. Ltd. back cover (stairs), 4, 5, 16, 113 (right)
Murat Taner/zefa/Corbis 48–49
Nick John 52 (top)
Pablo Corral Vega/Corbis 171
Park Hotel Tokyo back cover (dish)
Paul A. Souders/Corbis 34 (below)
Paul Chesley/National Geographic Image Collection 33 (below)
Paul Shackleford 18 (below), 96, 102, 111 (below)
Peter M. Wilson/Corbis 98
Photographer's Choice/Getty Images 109 (top)
Pierre Boussel/AFP/Getty Images 112 (below)
Pola Museum of Art 178, 179 (above)
Prada front flap (top), 105 (left)
Rainer Hackenberg/zefa/Corbis 181 (below)
Richard I'Anson/Getty Images 36 (top)
Richard Klune/Corbis 94
Ryan McVay/Getty Images 29
SCAI The Bathhouse back cover (below right), 31 (below)
Sisse Brimberg/National Geographic Image Collection 20 (below)
So Iwasaki front cover (glass structure), 19 (top), 21, 40 (below), 100 (left + right), 101 (above), 103, 114 (left)
Staffan Widstrand/Corbis 30 (below)
Steve Vidler/Photolibrary 19 (below)
Steve West/Getty Images 25
Tim Laman/National Geographic Image Collection 184 (left)
Vincent Sung/Studio 504 back cover (mobile), 37 (below), 41 (left), 109 (below), 114 (right), 179 (below), 197 (top)
Warwick Kent/Photolibrary 37 (top)
Wholly Owned Cayman/Getty Images 8–9
Yeon Soo Kim/Studio 504 51 (below), 53, 198 (top)

The publishers would like to thank Takeshi Goto, Paul Jackson, Yoshihiro Murata, Mitsuhiro Oda and Kodansha International for their help and support during the production of this book.

directory

HOTELS

Conrad Tokyo (page 54)
1-9-1 Higashi-Shinbashi, Minato-ku,
Tokyo, 105-7337
telephone : +81.3.6388 8000
facsimile : +81.3.6388 8001
tokyoinfo@conradhotels.com
www.conradhotels.com

Four Seasons Hotel Tokyo at Chinzan-so
(page 116)
2-10-8, Sekiguchi, Bunkyo-ku,
Tokyo, 112-8667
telephone : +81.3.3943 6958
facsimile : +81.3.3943 1255
tokyo.concierge@fourseasons.com
www.fourseasons/tokyo

Four Seasons Hotel Tokyo at Marunouchi
(page 56)
Pacific Century Place, 1-11-1 Marunouchi,
Chiyoda-ku, Tokyo, 100-6277
telephone : +81.3.5222 7222
facsimile : +81.3.5222 1255
reservations.mar@fourseasons.com
www.fourseasons.com

Grand Hyatt Tokyo (page 118)
6-10-3 Roppongi, Minato-ku, Tokyo, 106-0032
telephone : +81.3.4333 1234
facsimile : +81.3.4333 8123
info@tyogh.com
www.tokyo.grand.hyatt.com

Gora Kadan (page 202)
1300 Gora Hakone-machi, Ashigara-shimogun,
Kanagawa-ken, 250-0408
telephone : +81.460.23331
facsimile : +81.460.23334
info@gorakadan.com
www.gorakadan.com

Hotel Granvia Kyoto (page 204)
901 Higashi Shiokoji-cho, Shiokoji-sagaru,
Karasuma-dori, Shimogyo-ku, Kyoto, 600-8216
telephone : +81.75.344 8888
facsimile : +81.75.344 4400
hotel@granvia-kyoto.co.jp
www.granvia-kyoto.co.jp

Hyatt Regency Hakone Resort + Spa
(page 200)
1320 Gora Hakone-machi, Ashigarashimo-gun,
Kanagawa, 250-0408
telephone : +81.460.822 000
facsimile : +81.460.822 001
reservations.hakone@hyattintl.com
www.hakone.regency.hyatt.com

Hyatt Regency Kyoto (page 206)
644-2 Sanjusangendo-mawari,
Higashiyama-ku, Kyoto, 605-0941
telephone : +81.75.541 1234
facsimile : +81.75.541 2203
info@hyattregencykyoto.com
www.kyoto.regency.hyatt.com

Mandarin Oriental, Tokyo (page 58)
2-1-1 Nihonbashi-Muromachi, Chuo-ku,
Tokyo, 103-8328
telephone : +81.3.3270 8800
facsimile : +81.3.3270 8828
motyo-reservations@mohg.com
www.mandarinoriental.com/tokyo

Park Hotel Tokyo (page 60)
Shiodome Media Tower, 1-7-1 Higashi-
Shimbashi, Minato-ku, Tokyo, 105-7227
telephone : +81.3.6252 1111
facsimile : +81.3.6252 1001
info@parkhoteltokyo.com
www.parkhoteltokyo.com

The Peninsula Tokyo (page 62)
1-8-1 Yurakucho, Chiyoda-ku,
Tokyo, 100-0006
telephone : +81.3.6270 2888
facsimile : +81.3.6270 2000
ptk@peninsula.com
www.peninsula.com/tokyo

The Ritz-Carlton, Tokyo (page 120)
Tokyo Midtown, 9-7-1 Akasaka, Minato-ku,
Tokyo, 107-6245
telephone : +81.3.3423 8000
facsimile : +81.3.3423 8001
www.ritzcarlton.com

The Westin Tokyo (page 122)
1-4-1 Mita, Meguro-ku,
Tokyo, 153-8580
telephone : +81.3.5423 7000
facsimile : +81.3.5423 7600
wetok@westin.com
www.westin.com

RESTAURANTS

Beige Alain Ducasse Tokyo (page 64)
10F Chanel Ginza Building, 3-5-3 Ginza,
Chuo-ko, Tokyo, 104-0061
telephone : +81.3.5159 5500
facsimile : +81.3.5159 5501
info@beige-tokyo.com
www.beige-tokyo.com

Citabria (page 125)
2-26-4 Nishi-Azabu, Minato-ku,
Tokyo, 106-0031
telephone : +81.3.5766 9500
facsimile : +81.3.5766 9501
info@citabria.co.jp
www.citabria.co.jp

Den Aquaroom Aoyama (page 126)
B1 FIK Minami-Aoyama Building,
5-13-3 Minami-Aoyama, Minato-ku,
Tokyo, 107-0062
telephone : +81.3.5778 2090
facsimile : +81.3.5778 2096
aqua.aoyama@my.sgn.ne.jp
www.myuplanning.com

Furutoshi (page 128)
1, 2F Park View Nishi-Azabu,
1-15-10 Nishi-Azabu, Minato-ku,
Tokyo, 106-0031
telephone : +81.3.5775 1275
facsimile : +81.3.5775 1276
info@furutoshi.com
www.furutoshi.com

Grand Hyatt Restaurants (page 130)
Grand Hyatt Tokyo, 6-10-3 Roppongi,
Minato-ku, Tokyo, 106-0032
telephone : +81.3.4333 1234
facsimile : +81.3.4333 8123
info@tyogh.com
www.tokyo.grand.hyatt.com

Il Pinolo (page 66)
9F Ginza Green, 7-8-7 Ginza, Chuo-ku,
Tokyo, 104-0061
telephone : +81.3.5537 0474
facsimile : +81.3.5537 0475
ilpinolo2@stillfoods.com
www.il-pinolo.com

Kurayamizaka Miyashita Restaurants
(page 132)
2-24-8 Minami-Aoyama, Minato-ku,
Tokyo, 107-0062
telephone/facsimile: +81.3.5785 2431
kmacky@ds-miyashita.jp
www.ds-miyashita.jp

L'Osier (page 68)
7-5-5 Ginza, Chuo-ku, Tokyo, 104-8010
telephone : +81.3.3571 6050
facsimile : +81.3.3571 6080
www.shiseido.co.jp/e/losier/index.htm

le 6eme sens d'OENON (page 70)
6-2-10, Ginza, Chuo-ku,
Tokyo, 104-0061
telephone : +81.3.3575 2767
facsimile : +81.3.3289 5937
www.6eme.com

Mango Tree Tokyo (page 72)
35F Marunouchi Building, 2-4-1 Marunouchi,
Chiyoda-ku, Tokyo, 100-6335
telephone : +81.3.5224 5489
facsimile : +81.3.5224 5525
info@wonderland.to
website: www.mangotree.jp

My Humble House Tokyo (page 74)
1-9-1 Higashi-Shinbashi, Minato-ku,
Tokyo, 105-7337
telephone : +81.3.6388 8000
facsimile : +81.3.6388 8001
tokyoinfo@conradhotels.com
www.conradhotels.com

Pacific Currents (page 134)
2F Marto Building, 2-20-7 Azabu-Juban,
Minato-ku, Tokyo, 106-0045
telephone : +81.3.5765 2356
facsimile : +81.3.5765 2357
info@pacificcurrents.com
www.pacificcurrents.com

Roti (page 136)
1F Piramide Building, 6-6-9 Roppongi, Minato-
ku, Tokyo 106-0230
telephone : +81.3.5785 3671
facsimile : +81.3.5785 3672
info@rotico.com
www.rotico.com

Sky (page 76)
16F Mitsui Garden Hotel, 8-13-1 Ginza,
Chuo-ku, Tokyo, 104-0061
telephone : +81.3.3543 3157
facsimile : +81.3.3543 3158
info@sky-ginza.com
www.sky-ginza.com

Stair (page 138)
2F, 5-5-1, Minamiaoyama, Minato-ku,
Tokyo, 107-0062
telephone : +81.3.5778 3773
facsimile : +81.3.5778 3773
stair@air.ocn.ne.jp
www.stair-lounge.com

Super Dining Zipangu (page 140)
14F Akasaka Excel Hotel, 2-14-3 Nagatacho,
Chiyoda-ku, Tokyo, 100-0014
telephone : +81.3.3580 3661
facsimile : +81.3.3589 3112
zipangu@nadaman.co.jp
www.nadaman.co.jp

The Oregon Bar + Grill (page 78)
42F Shiodome City Centre, 1-5-2 Higashi-
Shimbashi, Minato-ku, Tokyo, 105-7142
telephone : +81.3.6215 8585
facsimile : +81.3.6215 8586
info@wonderland.to
www.wonderland.to

SHOPS

Atelier Shinji (page 80)
5-13-11 Ginza, Chuo-ku, Tokyo, 104-0061
telephone : +81.3.5565 5950
facsimile : +81.3.5565 9771
info@ateliershinji.com
www.ateliershinji.com

Badou-R (page 142)
7-7-21 Minami-Aoyama, Minato-ku,
Tokyo, 107-0062
telephone : +81.3.5778 0045
facsimile : +81.3.3498 9945
shop-badour@45rpm.co.jp
www.45rpm.jp

Dresscamp (page 144)
2-33-12-503 Jingumae, Shibuya-ku,
Tokyo, 150-0001
telephone : +81.3.3423 1279
facsimile : +81.3.3423 0826
www.dresscamp.org

Fuji-Torii (page 146)
6-1-10 Jingumae, Shibuya-ku,
Tokyo, 150-0001
telephone : +81.3.3400 2777
facsimile : +81.3.3400 5777
www.fuji-torii.com

Fukumitsuya (page 82)
1F, 5-5-8 Ginza, Chuo-ku,
Tokyo, 104-0061
telephone : +81.3.3569 2291
facsimile : +81.3.3569 2291
ginza@fukumitsuya.co.jp
www.fukumitsuya.co.jp

Issey Miyake Aoyama (page 148)
3-18-11 Minami-Aoyama, Minato-ku,
Tokyo, 107-0062
telephone : +81.3.3423 1408
www.isseymiyake.com

Ito-ya (page 84)
3-18-11 Minami-Aoyama, Minato-ku,
Tokyo, 107-0062
telephone : +81.3.3423 1408
www.isseymiyake.com

Mizuma Art Gallery (page 150)
2F Fujiya Building, 1-3-9 Kamimeguro,
Meguro-ku, Tokyo, 153-0051
telephone : +81.3.3793 7931
facsimile : +81.3.3793 7887
gallery@mizuma-art.co.jp
www.mizuma-art.com

Omotesando Hills (page 152)
4-12-10 Jingumae, Shibuya-ku,
Tokyo, 150-0001
telephone : +81.3.3497 0310
www.omotesandohills.com

Pleats Please Issey Miyake Aoyama
(page 156)
La Place Minami Aoyama, 3-13-21 Minami-
Aoyama, Minato-ku, Tokyo, 107-0062
telephone : +81.3.5772 7750
www.isseymiyake.com

Roppongi Hills (page 158)
Direct link by concourse to Roppongi Station
Mori Art Museum : +81.3.5777 8600
Tokyo City View : +81.3.6406 6652
Roppongi Hills Tours : +81.3.6406 6677
www.roppongihills.com

SCAI The Bathhouse (page 86)
6-1-23 Yanaka, Taito-ku,
Tokyo, 110-0001
telephone : +81.3.3821 1144
facsimile : +81.3.3821 3553
info@scaithebathhouse.com
www.scaithebathhouse.com

Tasaki Shinju (page 88)
5-7-5, Ginza, Chuo-ku,
Tokyo, 104-8010
telephone : +81.3.5561 8879
facsimile : +81.3.5561 0748
www.tasaki.co.jp

Yojiya (page 210)
538 Ichinofunairi-cho, Nijo-sagaru,
Kawaramachi-dori, Nakagyo-ku,
Kyoto, 604-0924
telephone : +81.75.253 1707
facsimile : +81.75.253 1708
www.yojiya.co.jp

SPAS

NAGOMI Spa and Fitness (page 164)
5F Grand Hyatt Tokyo, 6-10-3 Roppongi,
Minato-ku, Tokyo, 106-0032
telephone : +81.3.4333 1234
facsimile : +81.3.4333 8123
info@tyogh.com
www.tokyo.grand.hyatt.com

The Spa at Mandarin Oriental, Tokyo
(page 90)
Mandarin Oriental, Tokyo, 2-1-1 Nihonbashi-
Muromachi, Chuo-ku, Tokyo, 103-8328
telephone : +81.3.3270 8800
facsimile : +81.3.3270 8828
motyo-reservations@mohg.com
www.mandarinoriental.com/tokyo

YU, The Spa (page 166)
Four Seasons Hotel Tokyo at Chinzan-so,
2-10-8, Sekiguchi, Bunkyo-ku,
Tokyo, 112-8667
telephone : +81.3.3943 6958
facsimile : +81.3.3943 1255
tokyo.concierge@fourseasons.com
www.fourseasons.com/tokyo

AIRLINES

Japan Airlines (page 212)
UK reservations : 0845 774 7700
Japan reservations: 0120 25 5931
www.jal.com